Hurricane Mitch Reconstruction/Gulf of Fonseca Contaminant Survey and Assessment

I0438644

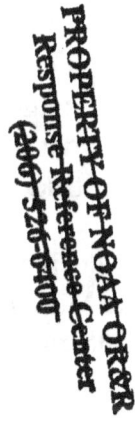
Mary Baker Matta
David McKinnie
Office of Response and Restoration
NOAA Ocean Service
Seattle, Washington

Enrique Barraza
El Salvador Ministry of the Environment
and Natural Resources
San Salvador

Jose Sericano
Texas A&M University
College Station, Texas

May 2002

National Oceanic and Atmospheric Administration
Weather Bureau Hurricane Series

ERRATA NOTICE

Table of Contents

Acknowledgments

The contributions of the following individuals, who made this project a success, are gratefully acknowledged

César Funes Abrego
Maria Mercedes Alonzo
José Luis Avila
Roxanna Bulnes
Mario Callejas
Héctor Luis Corrales
Peter Crumley
Gary Cummings
Andrés Diaz
Lisa DiPinto
Larry Drazba
Monica Drazba
Jim Farr
Martín Flütsch Caracas
Lara Garcia Fogarty
Jo Gardiner
Elizabeth Gonzalez
Margaret Harritt
Peter Hearn
David Hughes
José Luis Iglesias
Ed Johnson
Herberth Enrique Lopez
Saúl Antonio Montufar
Edas Muòoz
José Antonio Núòez
Adrian Oviedo
Judith Panameòo
Juan José Paniagua
Osmin Pocasaugre
David Atilio Ramirez
Julio Rene López Ramirez
Agnés Saborío Coze
Pilar Thorn
Leyla M. de Umaòa
José Manuel Vargas
Miguel Angel Vásquez
Néstor Windevoxhel Lora
Alberto Zelaya
Calina Zepeda

Please cite as:
Matta, Mary Baker, David McKinnie, Enrique Barraza, and Jose Sericano. 2002.
Hurricane Mitch reconstruction/Gulf of Fonseca contaminant survey and assessment.
Seattle: Office of Response and Restoration, NOAA Ocean Service. 46pp.

1.0 Background, Goals, and Objectives

Hurricane Mitch had severe effects on the environment and industry of Central America. In October 1998 the storm dropped between one and six inches of rain on the region within a six day period, killing 11,000 people, destroying homes of 3 million people, and destroying 70 percent of the transportation infrastructure in Honduras. Farms and facilities were destroyed, the Rio Choluteca temporarily changed course, erosion and flooding released tons of sediment to downstream areas, pesticides and other farm chemicals were swept from storage depots into the Gulf, and DDT and other persistent chemicals may have been mobilized from soil or sediment into watersheds that drain into the Gulf. Shrimp aquaculture facilities that surround the Gulf of Fonseca were severely affected by flooding, erosion, and deposition of sediments. After the hurricane, low concentrations of pesticides were detected in shrimp, and white spot disease was confirmed to be present in shrimp ponds in Nicaragua. The hurricane may have increased chemical contamination in the area and made shrimp more susceptible to viruses and other diseases.

As part of the U.S. Government assistance to Honduras, Nicaragua, El Salvador, and Guatemala following the hurricane, NOAA (in partnership with other U.S. government and local counterpart agencies) conducted a baseline survey of the extent and distribution of contaminants in the Gulf of Fonseca, its estuaries, and surrounding areas. Better knowledge of coastal ecosystems, including human health and environmental threats caused by contaminants mobilized by Hurricane Mitch, will provide the information needed to implement sustainable, resilient management practices for natural resources. Ultimately, effective management practices could minimize economic and environmental consequences of severe storms.

The goal of the contaminant assessment and survey was to improve understanding of natural processes in the Gulf of Fonseca and their relationship to industrial, yet sustainable, uses of the natural environment (e.g., shrimp aquaculture), artisans, and subsistence.

Project objectives:
- Determine the distribution of contaminants in Gulf of Fonseca surface water and tributaries after the first large storms of the rainy season.
- Determine the distribution and magnitude of contaminants in sediment, fish, and crabs from the Gulf of Fonseca
- Identify likely source areas for contamination around the Gulf of Fonseca
- Recommend sustainable monitoring of contaminants
- Deliver data and information useful for watershed management

2.0 Methods
2.1 Sample Collection Methods

2.1.1 Water-sampling method

2.1.1.1. Sample timing
It is logistically difficult to synchronize sampling to a constant tidal phase. We minimized the effects of tidal variability by sampling just after the first large storm of the rainy season, preferably near the lowest low tide of the month. We sampled stations located within the area of influence of tides from the Gulf of Fonseca during outgoing tides to maximize the probability that runoff from upstream areas was collected.

Samples were collected in May and June 2000. Sampling in El Salvador took place on June 13 and June 14, 2000. In Honduras, samples were collected between June 5 and June 8, 2000. Samples in Nicaragua were collected between May 29 and June 2, 2000.

2.1.1.2. Sample locations
Surface water of the central channel of watercourses was a priority for sampling. This approach integrated inputs of contaminants from upstream, input from adjacent lateral shoals, contributions of localized discharges, and contaminants present within the local water column. Samples taken by boat were collected from the surface water of the central channel of the selected waterways. Samples were collected from the bow of the boat, with the bow facing upstream (away from the influence of outboard motors). Stations accessible from roads were located upstream of roads or bridges to minimize effects of road runoff. These stations were biased toward the bank that most likely represented a depositional area for sediment.

Table 1 lists the stations where water samples were collected. Twelve stations were sampled in El Salvador; 24 stations were sampled in Honduras; and 25 stations were sampled in Nicaragua, for a total of 61 sampling locations around the Gulf of Fonseca (Figure 1).

2.1.1.3. Water sample collection and processing methods
Before the sample was collected, we obtained and recorded global positioning system (GPS) coordinates for the station. We made notes regarding quality and condition of the sediment, vegetation, and presence of biota (especially fiddler crabs and bivalves), recording date, time, tidal stage, and anything unusual about the station.

Two approaches were used to collect water samples: small streams accessible by road were sampled by wading into shallow water from shore; other stations were accessed from small boats.

Samples were collected from 0.3 m below the surface, directly into pre-cleaned jars purchased from Eagle-Picher, Miami, Oklahoma. The following sample collection procedure was used:

- Latex gloves were worn by people collecting samples
- Smoking was not allowed while samples were being collected

- One sample consisted of four 1-L jars of water (two plastic bottles for trace metals and suspended sediments; two glass bottles for organochlorine/polynuclear aromatic hydrocarbons and organophosphate pesticides)
- If the station served as an interlaboratory validation station, a total of four samples (16 jars of water) were collected
- Each sampling jar was submerged with the lid on
- The lid of the jar was removed while holding it under water
- Care was taken to avoid surface slicks and large floating or suspended objects
- When the jar was full, it was capped and then removed from the water
- The outside of the jar was dried
- Each bottle was labeled with the station number, date, and time

Chemical analyses for metals and pesticides was performed by one local lab in each of the three countries, with verification analyses and polynuclear aromatic hydrocarbon (PAH) analyses for a subset of samples for each country performed in the United States by Texas A&M University's Geochemical and Environmental Research Group. Therefore, at three stations in each of the three countries (for a total of nine stations), we collected four replicate water samples. Replicate samples were sent to each of the four labs to compare results.

After samples were collected, these procedures were followed to process the samples:
- Labels were wrapped with clear tape
- Glass jars were wrapped in bubble wrap
- Each jar was placed in a Ziploc bag and sealed
- Jars were placed on ice in a cooler
- Within several hours, 2 ml of ACS reagent grade hydrochloric acid (HCl) was added to each jar to preserve the sample
- The lid of each jar was then sealed with electrical tape (all jars from the same station were sealed with the same color tape)

Samples were kept chilled at all times in coolers full of ice. Overnight mail couriers delivered samples shipped out of the country. Other samples were delivered to the laboratory every few days.

2.1.2. Sediment sampling methods

2.1.2.1. Sample Timing
Analysis of sediment can provide an integrated picture of contamination over time, which makes the timing of sample collection less critical. Sediment samples were collected at the same time as biota samples were taken. Samples were collected in El Salvador between October 15 and October 19, 2000. In Honduras, samples were collected between January 11 and January 27, 2001. Nicaraguan samples were collected between February 25, and March 8, 2001.

2.1.2.2. Sediment Sample Locations
Most of the stations sampled for water were also sampled for sediments. Sediment stations were biased towards the stream banks, the most likely depositional areas for sediment.

Table 1 lists stations where we collected sediment samples. Fifty-five stations were sampled for sediment throughout the Gulf of Fonseca area. Ten stations were located in El Salvador, 22 stations were located in Honduras, and 23 stations were located in Nicaragua (Figure 1).

2.1.2.3. Sediment Sample Collection and processing methods

Two methods were used to access sampling stations: small streams that are accessible by road were sampled by wading into shallow water from shore; other stations were accessed from small boats.

Before the sample was collected, we obtained and recorded GPS coordinates, temperature, and salinity for the station. We noted quality and condition of the sediment, vegetation, presence of biota, date, time, tidal stage, and anything unusual about the station.

Decontamination procedures were conducted between stations and completed before new samples were collected.

Surface sediment samples were collected (with the surface defined as sediment depth from 0-10 cm). At stations accessible by road, samples were collected by hand with a stainless steel trowel from shallow water. At stations accessible only by boat, samples were collected using a hand-held, petit-ponar sampler. Composite sediment samples were obtained at each station by combining three discrete sediment samples from three separate locations spaced up to 50 m apart. Specific sample collection procedures included:

- Latex gloves were worn by people collecting samples;
- Smoking was not allowed while samples were collected;
- Sediment collected by trowels or sampler was placed into a stainless steel bowl. Sediments from three grabs or three individual locations were combined into one sample.
- The sample was mixed thoroughly with a stainless steel spoon.
- One sample consisted of one 16-oz glass jar for organic contaminants; one 8-oz glass jar for metals; one Ziploc bag for sediment grain size analysis
- If the station was to serve as an inter-laboratory validation station, a total of four split samples (four 16-oz jars and four 8-oz jars) were collected;
- The outside of each jar was dried, labeled with the station number, date, and time, and wrapped with clear tape
- The lid of the jar was sealed with electrical tape (all jars from the same station were sealed with the same color tape)
- Glass jars were wrapped in bubble wrap, placed in a Ziploc bag and sealed and placed on ice in a cooler.
- Samplers, trowels, spoons, and bowls were decontaminated between stations by scrubbing with a brush, rinsing with site water, rinsing with an Alconox detergent solution, and a final rinse with water from the next station.

Chemical analyses for metals and pesticides was performed by a local labs in each of the three countries, with verification analyses and PAH analyses for a subset of samples for each country performed in the United States by Texas A&M University's Geochemical and Environmental Research Group. Therefore, at three stations in each of the three countries (for a total of nine stations), four replicate sediment samples were collected. Replicate samples were sent to each of the four labs to compare results.

Samples were kept chilled at all times in coolers full of ice. Overnight mail couriers delivered samples shipped out of the country. Other samples were delivered to the laboratory every few days.

2.1.3 Biota sampling methods

2.1.3.1 Species selection and timing

Analysis of biota can serve to provide an integrated picture of contamination over time. Chemical analysis of resident organisms indicates whether contaminants found in sediment or water are available for uptake by animals or humans, and can integrate long-term exposure conditions. Concentrations in biota can vary seasonally, and for some contaminants (for example, mercury), concentrations peak at the end of summer (Beckvar et al.1996). Sampling for biota in the Gulf of Fonseca took place over the fall and winter of 2000-2001.

Fiddler crabs (*Uca* spp.) were selected as a target species because they are widely distributed throughout the downstream areas of the Gulf of Fonseca and its estuaries. They burrow in sediment in mudflats adjacent to mangroves and remain within a small home range. Concentrations in whole crabs (including the carapace) serve as an indicator of whether contaminants in sediments are potentially available to higher trophic levels, including fish, birds, and humans.

A variety of fish species are harvested from the Gulf of Fonseca and its estuaries. Most fish is consumed locally. Catfish (*Bagre panamensis* and *Arius seemani* –formerly *Galeichthys jordani*) were selected as our target species due to their close association with sediment and human diet.

2.1.3.2 Sample locations

Fiddler crabs were collected from 39 downstream sediment-sampling stations in the Gulf of Fonseca and the adjacent estuaries. Table 1 lists stations where fiddler crabs were collected. Six stations were sampled for crabs in El Salvador; 19 stations were sampled in Honduras; and 14 locations were sampled for fiddler crabs in Nicaragua (Figure 1).

Fish were collected from a total of 14 stations in the Gulf of Fonseca. Fish sample locations are listed in Table 1. Composite samples were collected from five stations in El Salvador, six stations in Honduras, and three stations in Nicaragua.

2.1.3.3 Fiddler crab collection and processing methods

Fiddler crabs were collected at the same time and same locations as the sediment samples. Samples were collected in El Salvador between October 15 and October 19, 2000. In Honduras, samples were collected between January 11 and January 27, 2001. Nicaraguan samples were collected between February 25 and March 8, 2001.

Fiddler crabs were collected by hand using trowels to trap fiddler crabs in their burrows in intertidal creek banks at the designated sampling stations. At these stations (comprised of three specific locations around each sampling station). a composite crab tissue sample consisted of at least 12 mature crabs of similar size and mixed sex. and contained approximately 35 g of tissue for analysis. Whole crabs (including the carapace) were analyzed.

- Fiddler crabs were collected during an incoming tide while they were actively feeding
- Crabs were washed in a bucket of water obtained from the site to remove adhering sediment
- Crabs were weighed, wrapped in decontaminated aluminum foil. and placed in Ziploc bags.
- Each sample consisted of 35 g of whole crabs. At each replicate station, four 35g split samples will be collected.
- To create samples, crabs were sorted by species (using carapace characteristics)
- Crab samples were weighed, and sorted into 35 g composite samples.
- Samples were wrapped in pre-cleaned foil and placed in labeled zip-loc bags
- Bags were placed on ice in a cooler
- Spoons, and buckets were decontaminated between stations by scrubbing with a brush. rinsing with site water, rinsing with an Alconox detergent solution. and a final rinse with water from the next station. Sample processing equipment was cleaned with Alconox and fresh water between samples.

Chemical analyses for metals and pesticides was performed by a local lab in each of the three countries. with verification analyses and PAH analyses for a subset of samples for each country performed in the United States by Texas A&M University's Geochemical and Environmental Research Group. Therefore, at three stations in each of the three countries (for a total of nine stations), four replicate crab samples were collected. Replicate samples were sent to each of the four labs to compare results.

Samples were kept chilled at all times in coolers full of ice. Samples shipped out of the country were delivered to overnight mail couriers. Other samples were delivered to the laboratory every few days.

2.1.3.4 Fish collection and processing method

Resident catfish samples were collected at the same time as fiddler crab and sediment samples but at only a few designated stations. Fish were collected by local fishermen using gillnets or throw-nets within sight of sediment-sampling stations. At these stations, one composite fish tissue sample generally consisted of at least three fish. Fish sizes and weights were measured and recorded.

- Fish were rinsed in a bucket of site water to remove sediment
- Whole fish were weighed and measured
- Whole fish were cleaned and sectioned into skin-on filets of similar size
- If four replicate samples were created from a composite of fish. each filet was divided into four portions, with one portion used to create each composite sample.

- Each sample consisted of 35 g of fish filets (composited from at least three individual fish). At each replicate station, four 35-g samples were collected.
- Samples were weighed and wrapped in pre-cleaned foil
- Each packet was placed in a Ziploc bag and seal
- Samples were placed on ice in a cooler
- Buckets and dip nets were decontaminated between stations by scrubbing with a brush, rinsing with site water, rinsing with an Alconox detergent solution, and a final rinse with water from the next station. Sample processing equipment (knives, scalpels, scale, cutting boards) was cleaned with Alconox and fresh water between samples.

Chemical analyses for metals and pesticides was performed by a local lab in each of the three countries, with verification analyses and PAH analyses for a subset of samples for each country performed in the United States by Texas A&M University's Geochemical and Environmental Research Group. Therefore, at three stations in each of the three countries (for a total of nine stations), four replicate fish samples were collected. Replicate samples were sent to each of the four labs to compare results.

Samples were kept chilled at all times in coolers full of ice. Samples shipped out of the country were delivered to overnight mail couriers. Other samples were delivered to the laboratory every few days.

2.2 Quality assurance methods

Laboratories in each country conducted chemical analyses. To ensure that results from each laboratory were comparable, Texas A&M University conducted training and purchased equipment for chemical analysis in each country. Training emphasized basic procedures as well as the importance of quality assurance/quality control.

The Laboratorio Nacional de Residuos Biologicos MAG (MAGFOR) conducted analysis in Nicaragua, the Centro de Estudios y Control de Contaminantes (CESCCO) conducted analysis in Honduras, and the Fundacion Salvadorena para el Desarrollo Economico y Social (FUSADES, a non-profit laboratory) conducted analysis in El Salvador. All laboratories included analysis of quality assurance/quality control samples, including duplicate samples, standard reference materials for sediment and fish, matrix spike samples, and matrix spike duplicate samples.

The three laboratories also participated in inter-laboratory calibration exercises, which included analysis of replicate water, sediment, fish and crab samples from three stations in each country. Texas A&M University analyzed an additional replicate sample from each country for comparison.

2.3 Chemical Analysis Methods

The methods described here are those followed by the Texas A&M laboratory. Other labs followed these methods with minor modifications.

2.3.1 Chlorinated Pesticides and PAHs

The analytical procedure for the analysis of chlorinated pesticides and polynuclear aromatic hydrocarbons (PAHs) is based on a method developed by MacLeod (1985) as modified by Wade et al. 1988 and Sericano et al. 1990. Approximately 20 g of dried sediment were extracted with an accelerated solvent extraction (ASE) technique using methylene chloride. Approximately 5 g of wet tissue were extracted with methylene chloride using a homogenizer (Tekmar Tissumizer) after adding anhydrous sodium sulfate. The extracts were fractionated by alumina:silica gel (80-100 mesh) chromatography. The extracts were eluted from the column with a 1:1 pentane-methylene chloride mixture and concentrated to 1 mL in hexane for instrumental analysis. Pesticides were analyzed by gas chromatography in the splitless mode using an electron capture detector (ECD). A 30 m x 0.25 mm i.d. fused-silica column with DB-5 bonded phase (J&W Scientific, Inc.) provided component separations. Four calibration solutions were used to generate a calibration curve. The surrogates DBOFB (4,4'-dibromooctafluorobiphenyl), PCB 103 and PCB 198 were added to the samples before extraction. The internal standard, TCMX (tetrachloro-m-xylene), was added prior to GC/ECD analysis. The chromatographic conditions were $100^{o}C$ for 1 min, then $5^{o}C$ min^{-1} until $140^{o}C$, hold for 1 min, then $1.5^{o}C$ min^{-1} to $250^{o}C$, hold for 1 min, and then $10^{o}C$ min^{-1} to a final temperature of $300^{o}C$, which was held for 5 min.

Aromatic hydrocarbons were quantified by gas chromatography with mass spectrometric (GC/MS) detection (HP-5890 and HP-5970-MSD) in the selected ion mode (SIM). The samples were injected in the splitless mode into a 30 m x 0.25 mm (0.32 μm film thickness), DB-5 fused silica capillary column (J&W Scientific, Inc.) at an initial temperature of $60°C$ and temperature programmed at $12^{o}C$ min^{-1} to $300^{o}C$ and held at the final temperature for six minutes. The mass spectral data were acquired and the molecular ions for each of the PAH analytes were used for quantification. The GC/MS was calibrated by injecting standards at five concentrations. Analyte identification was based on the retention time of the quantitation ion for each analyte and a series of confirmation ions. Deuterated aromatic compounds were used as surrogates and internal standards.

2.3.2 Organophosphorous Pesticides
The tissue and sediment samples were extracted with an accelerated solvent extractor (ASE) technique using methylene chloride after adding anhydrous sodium sulfate to dry the sample. Lipids were removed from the extracts using gel permeation chromatography. Organophosphorous pesticides were quantified by GC/MS detection (HP-5890 and HP-5970-MSD) in the selected ion mode (SIM). The samples were injected in the splitless mode into a 30 m x 0.25 mm (0.32 μm film thickness) DB-5 fused silica capillary column (J&W Scientific, Inc.) at an initial temperature of $100°C$ and temperature programmed at $10^{o}C$ min^{-1} to $200^{o}C$, then at $5^{o}C$ min^{-1} to 300 and held at the final temperature for 3 min. Analyte identification was based on the retention time of the quantitation ion for each analyte and a series of confirmation ions.

2.3.3 Trace Metals
Arsenic, cadmium, lead, and selenium were analyzed by atomic absorption spectrophotommetry by flame or graphite furnace (GFAA/FAA. Copper, nickel, and zinc were analyzed by inductively coupled plasma optical emission spectrometry (ICP-OES). Mercury was analyzed by cold vapor atomic absorption spectrometry (CVAA). Briefly, tissue samples were lyophilized, ground to a fine powder, and homogenized. The homogenized tissues were then dissolved in concentrated nitric acid. Sediment samples were lyophilized and fractions <63 μm separated by nylon sieves. For sediment sample digestion about 0.1 to 0.3 grams of the <63 μm fractions were extracted in closed Teflon bombs with aqua regia.

Mercury was determined by U.S. Environmental Protection Agency (EPA) method 245.5 with minor revisions (EPA, 1980). For sediments a 0.5- to 1.0-gram sample (dry weight; dw) was used. For tissues a 1.5- to 2.0-gram sample (wet weight) was used. Briefly, the samples were weighed into a 50-ml polypropylene centrifuge tube. Concentrated sulfuric and nitric acids were added and the samples heated in a water bath. After cooling distilled water, potassium permanganate, and potassium persulfate were added to each tube. The samples were returned to the water bath. After cooling, hydroxylamine hydrochloride was added to reduce excess permanganate. Mercury was determined by a modification of the method of Hatch and Ott (1968). A portion of the digest solution was placed in a sealed container with stannous chloride. Mercury was reduced to the elemental state and aerated from solution into an atomic absorption spectrophotometer where its concentration was measured. Reagent blanks and standard reference materials (SRMs) were prepared and digested for each batch of samples as part of the laboratory internal QA/QC procedures.

2.4 Methods for evaluating potential sources and concentrations

Data from this study were evaluated to determine potential contaminant sources and to investigate implications of contaminant concentrations for human health and ecological concerns. Contaminant sources were evaluated by mapping data, then examining contaminant distributions to determine gradients, areas with elevated concentrations, and areas representing unusually low levels of contamination compared to other stations in the Gulf of Fonseca. Tidal influence, known source areas such as agricultural and port areas, and other land use information were considered in identifying gradients and areas of concern.

Water concentrations were evaluated using EPA's ambient water quality criteria (USEPA 1995). Water quality criteria have been developed for both fresh and marine waters and to evaluate possible implications of both chronic (more than four days) and acute (24 hour) exposures. Since the Gulf of Fonseca is an estuarine area with a range of salinities, the lower of the marine or freshwater criteria was used to evaluate concentrations. Ambient water quality criteria are expected to prevent 95 percent of aquatic species from harm. Endpoints considered in developing the criteria include both mortality and sub-lethal effects. Water quality criteria used in this report are shown in Table 2.

Sediment concentrations were evaluated using NOAA sediment quality guidelines (Long and MacDonald, 1998). Sediment quality guidelines indicate the relative probability of toxicity to benthic organisms. Two screening concentrations are available for each contaminant. The Effects Range-Low (ERL) represents the concentration at which adverse effects would be expected ten percent of the time. The Effects Range-Medium (ERM) represents the concentration above which adverse effects would be expected 50 percent of the time. Exceeding guidelines for more than one chemical increases the probability of toxic effects. Sediment screening values used in this report are shown in Table 3.

Fish tissue concentrations were evaluated using U.S. Food and Drug Administration guidelines for human health (USFDA 2000). Action levels and tolerances represent limits at or above which FDA will take legal action to remove products from the market. The action level for mercury is 1 part per million (ppm) wet weight methyl mercury in the edible portion. The action level for DDT (5 ppm wet weight) is for residues of the above pesticides individually, or in combination.

Additional information on human health implications of fish concentrations is also available in the literature. A number of U.S states have released fish consumption advisories based on the scientific literature (especially based on concerns for developmental neurotoxicity; Marsh et al. 1981, Cox et al. 1989). A reference dose for humans based on these concerns might equate to 1 x 10-4 mg/kg-day of methyl mercury (USEPA 1997).

Additional information is also available in the scientific literature to evaluate the implications of fish tissue concentrations on fish health. For example, Matta et al. (2001) indicates that whole-body concentrations in excess of 0.2 ppm wet weight are associated with adverse effects (reproductive or behavioral problems). Concentrations as low as 0.07-0.34 ppm wet weight may affect sensitive bird populations that consume fish (USEPA 1997). These wet-weight concentrations equate to approximately 0.3-1.2 ppm dry weight (assuming a water content for fish of 75 percent). For DDT, concerns for sub-lethal effects might begin at 0.3 ppm wet weight in whole bodies (Beckvar, personal communication). This would be equivalent to about 1.2-ppm dry weight.

3.0 Results and Findings

3.1 Quality assurance for chemical analysis

Table 4 summarizes the results of the analysis of standard reference materials for tissue and sediment. Standard reference materials are samples prepared with certified concentrations of known organochlorine and trace elements. Results of analyses from each laboratory were judged to be questionable if they were outside of accepted limits in either direction from certified concentrations.

Based on the comparison of split sample analyses from different laboratories, it appears that the FUSADES lab had difficulty analyzing organophosphate compounds in water and tissue and organochlorines in water. The MAGFOR lab had difficulty analyzing organophosphate compounds in tissue and sediment samples and with metals in water. The CESCCO lab had difficulty analyzing organophosphates in water, sediment, and tissue samples and organochlorine compounds in water.

3.2 Results by contaminant

Project data is available in Microsoft® Excel ™ spreadsheets on compact disc as an appendix to this report. A database and mapping project based in ArcView™ and NOAA's Query Manager™ software) has also been created to query and display the contaminant data from this survey. A CD containing this database and mapping project is available upon request from the authors.

In order to run the database and mapping project, the most basic hardware requirements include:
- VGA or higher-resolution monitor
- Mouse (or trackball)
- Adobe® Acrobat® Reader for viewing .PDF extension files

In order to use Query Manager, your hardware system will require a personal computer with:
- 80386sx processor (or higher)
- Microsoft® Windows® 95/ 98/ 2000/ or NT 4.0

To use the ArcView GIS Project the requirements for a Windows system include:
- Pentium class PC
- ArcView 3.1 or higher
- 32 MB of RAM with minimum of 17 MB of virtual memory
- An additional 515 MB of hard drive space is needed if not running the project directly from a CD-ROM

Tables 5-9 give an overview of the data discussed in this report. Selected maps presenting data distributions are also described in the following sections.

3.2.1 Mercury

Table 5 presents results of analyses for mercury. Analysis of mercury in sediment and water appeared to be difficult for several of the laboratories, so only selected results are presented in maps. Highest concentrations of mercury in fish tissue were detected in El Salvador at Estero

El Tamarindo (station EF061-Figure 2). Concentrations in fish from this station exceeded 5 ppm dw (Table 5). Other areas with elevated mercury (exceeding 1 ppm dw) in fish include near Potosi (station NF011) and at Puerto Morazàn (station NF017) in the Estero Real in Nicaragua, and at the mouth of the Rio Choluteca (station HF037) in Honduras. Mercury concentrations in sediment are not elevated where fish concentrations are highest (Figure 3). Lowest levels of mercury in sediment were found in Rio Nacaome. Concentrations of mercury in fish from El Tamarindo in El Salvador exceed the FDA limit and concentrations associated with adverse effects to fish reproduction (Matta et al. 2001). These results indicate that mercury is bioavailable in the Gulf of Fonseca.Generally, more than 90 percent of mercury in fish tissue is in the form of methyl-mercury (Beckvar et al. 1996).

3.2.2 Arsenic

Results of analyses for arsenic are presented in Table 6. Highest concentrations of arsenic in crab were detected in the Estero El Pedregal in Honduras (station HF035), where concentrations exceeded 14 ppm dw (Figure 4). Stations in the Estero Real (Nicaragua), El Tamarindo (El Salvador), and Estero San Bernardo (Honduras) also exceeded 5 ppm dw in whole crab. The area where the Choluteca River changed course during Hurricane Mitch (stations HF043 and HF042 in Honduras) also had elevated concentrations of arsenic in crab.

Highest sediment concentrations of arsenic were found in the Estero El Pedregal and upstream areas (stations HF038, HF037, HF035, HF034, HF039, HF063, HF065), and in western Bahía Chismuyo (station HF050) in Honduras (Figure 5). The highest concentration was detected at the farthest upstream station (HF065), where the concentration exceeded 10 ppm dw. The highest concentrations detected in this study just slightly exceeded the lower sediment screening concentration (8.2 ppm dw).

Two of the laboratories had difficulty analyzing arsenic concentrations in water. Based on the results from the other two laboratories, the highest water concentrations were found in Estero El Pedregal (HF037-Figure 6). Elevated concentrations were also detected in the Estero Real, and at El Tamarindo (EF061). The highest water concentration detected in this study (14 ppb) was well below the chronic marine water quality criteria (36 ppb).

Based on the results of crab and sediment sampling, it appears that there is a source of arsenic upstream of Estero El Pedregal, and that this arsenic is bioavailable.

3.2.3 Copper

Table 7 describes results of analyses for copper. Highest concentrations of copper in fish were detected in western Bahía Chismuyo (HF050), where fish muscle contained 20 ppm dw (Figure 7). Concentrations in fish were also elevated in Bahía San Lorenzo (HF044, where the Choluteca River changed course during Hurricane Mitch), La Unión (EF057), Estero El Pedregal (HF037), and Estero Torecillas (NF024). Copper was also elevated in crab in Bahía San Lorenzo (HF044 and HF042; Figure 8), upstream in the Estero Real (NF018), and at the mouth of the Rio Nacaome (HF048). Highest concentrations of copper in crab exceeded 160 ppm dw.

One lab had difficulty detecting copper in water and sediment. Highest concentrations of copper in sediment were detected in El Salvador (where concentrations ranged up to 90 ppm dw), in the

Estero San Bernardo, and the Estero El Pedregal (Honduras) where concentrations ranged between 30 and 50 ppm dw, and in the Estero Real (stations NF013, NF017, NF024; Figure 9). The highest sediment concentrations exceeded the lower sediment screening value (35 ppm dw), but not the higher value (270 ppm dw).

Highest concentrations of copper in water were detected at the mouth of the Estero San Bernardo (stations HF030 and HF032) and at Cedeño in Honduras (HF036), where concentrations exceeded 140 ppb (Figure 10). Upstream portions of Estero El Pedregal (stations HF034 and HF035) and Estero Real in Nicaragua (NF024 and NF013) also had elevated concentrations. The area where the Rio Choluteca changed course also had elevated concentrations of copper in water (HF041, HF042, HF043). Concentrations of copper in water exceeded both the chronic and acute ambient water quality criteria, indicating that water is potentially toxic.

Based on the results of fish, sediment, and water sampling, there may be sources of copper upstream of the Estero Pedregal, Estero San Bernardo, and Estero Real, which are all shrimp aquaculture areas.

3.2.4 PAHs

Polynuclear aromatic hydrocarbons (PAHs) were analyzed in sediment and water by Texas A&M University (Table 8). Highest concentrations of PAHs in sediment were detected at San Lorenzo (404 ppb dw) in Honduras. Lowest concentrations in sediment were detected in the Rio Nacaome (HF047, HF048). All concentrations detected in sediment were below the lowest sediment-screening threshold (4022 ppb dw). Highest concentrations of PAHs in water were detected at the mouth of the Rio Choluteca (HF037) in Honduras (0.33 ppb).

3.2.5 total DDT

The most abundant chlorinated pesticide residues encountered in these samples were DDT and its metabolites DDE and DDD. Concentrations of total DDT (the sum of o-p' and p-p' isomers of DDT, DDE, and DDD) are presented in Table 9. Six individual isomers were summed to create a total DDT value. Only detected values were summed. Highest concentrations in fish were detected at La Unión (EF057), which exceeded 2 ppm (dw); Figure 11). Fish from San Lorenzo (HF046), El Tamarindo (EF061), and Estero Torecillas (NF024) also had elevated DDT.

Highest concentrations of total DDT in sediment were detected in El Salvador (Figure 12). Station EF056 had the highest concentration (118 ppb dw). Sediments from San Lorenzo (HF046), the mouth of the Rio Choluteca (HF037) and the Rio Posoltega (NP010) also had elevated total DDT concentrations (more than 20 ppb dw) when compared to other stations. Most concentrations were below the upper sediment screening concentration of 46 ppb dw, but above the lower sediment screening concentration (1.5 ppb dw).

One lab had difficulty detecting DDT in water. Highest concentrations of total DDT in water were detected at El Tamarindo in El Salvador (station EF061), where concentrations exceeded 100 ppb (Figure 13). Concentrations were also elevated near Potosi in Nicaragua (station NF011) and at Estero Torecillas (NF024). DDT was widely detected in water throughout the estuaries of the Gulf of Fonseca. Most concentrations detected in water exceeded both the lower and upper ambient water quality criteria for DDT.

Most of the DDT detected in sediment and tissue samples were in the form of p-p'DDE or p-p' DDD. It is generally accepted that increased percentages of DDT metabolites (DDE and DDD) in environmental samples reflect a decreased input of fresh DDT since DDE and DDD are relatively minor components in commercial DDT formulations. The predominance of DDE metabolites confirms the usage of DDT in the Gulf of Fonseca watershed.

3.2.6 Organophosphate pesticides
Two labs had difficulties detecting organophosphate compounds in samples. Five organophosphate compounds were evaluated in this study: diazinon, malathion, methyl parathion, ethyl parathion, and ethion. Concentrations of organophosphate compounds were elevated in fish or crab from several areas. Diazinon was elevated in fish from Bahía La Unión (station EF058), where concentrations exceeded 160 ppb dry weight. Diazinon in fish was also elevated at Potosi (station HF011), where the concentration was 99 ppb. Malathion was elevated in crabs from station HF063 in Estero El Pedregal (144 ppb). Parathion compounds were elevated in crabs from the Estero Real (NF023; 111 ppb) and in crabs and fish from La Unión (EF057) (87 and 98 ppb). Ethion concentrations were elevated in crabs from Bahía San Lorenzo (HF045; 145 ppb) and from the Estero Real (NF023; 111 ppb).

All five organophosphate compounds were detected in sediment at low concentrations, generally less than 6 ppb. Exceptions include malathion in the Rio Choluteca (station HF040; 23ppb) and parathion in Estero Torecillas (station NF024; 29 ppb).

Methyl parathion was the compound detected at highest concentrations in water. The maximum concentration of methyl parathion was detected at station EF052 in the Bahía La Unión (0.304 ppb). Concentrations at several other stations also exceeded the acute ambient water quality criteria for parathion (0.065 ppb), including Estero Torecillas (NF024), Estero Padre Ramos (NP002), and near Corinto (NP008).

3.3. Areas of Concern By Country
3.3.1 El Salvador
Based on the results of this study, there are two areas of concern in El Salvador. The El Tamarindo area (stations EF061 and EF062) showed elevated concentrations of mercury in fish, arsenic in crab and water, copper in sediment, and total DDT in fish and water. Bahía La Unión (stations EF057, EF056, EF058, EF052, EF054) showed elevated concentrations of copper in fish, crab, sediment, and water; and total DDT in fish and sediment. These results are consistent with those of a previous survey of trace elements in Bahía La Unión (Barraza and Carballeira 1998), which found that concentrations of copper and zinc were elevated in mussels and sediments sampled from La Unión. During the initial phase of the International Mussel Watch Program, DDT was detected in mussels from La Unión (11.9 ppb dw) and La Libertad (177 ppb dw-IMWC, 1995)

3.3.2 Honduras

Five areas of concern were identified in Honduras. At San Lorenzo (station HF046), concentrations of PAHs in sediment were higher than at other stations. Concentrations of total DDT in fish and sediment were also elevated at San Lorenzo. During the initial phase of the International Mussel Watch Program, DDT was detected in mussels from San Lorenzo (12 and 17.8 ppb dw) in 1991 (IMWC, 1995). In Bahía San Lorenzo where the Rio Choluteca changed course during Hurricane Mitch (stations HF043, HF042) showed elevated concentrations of arsenic in crab and sediment, and elevated copper in fish, crab, and water. Western Bahía Chismuyo (station HF050) had elevated concentrations of arsenic in sediment and copper in fish.

The shrimp aquaculture producing areas in Estero El Pedregal and Estero San Bernardo have a variety of contamination issues. In Estero El Pedregal mercury concentrations in fish; arsenic in crab, sediment, and water; copper in fish, sediment, and water; and total DDT in sediment were higher than in most other locations. It appears that the Estero El Pedregal is a source of arsenic and copper to the Gulf of Fonseca. In the Estero San Bernardo, arsenic concentrations in crab; copper in sediment and water; and total DDT in water were elevated. Copper and total DDT concentrations in water are potentially toxic to aquatic life in these estuaries.

It appears that the Rio Nacaome stations (HF047 and HF048) would serve as appropriate reference stations for the Gulf of Fonseca area. Both stations have low concentrations of mercury and PAH in sediment, low levels of DDT in sediment, low levels of copper in water and sediment, and low to moderate concentrations of arsenic in crab and sediment. The only concern about these stations is the elevated concentration of copper in crab from station HF048.

3.3.3 Nicaragua

In Nicaragua, two portions of the Estero Real are of concern. The Estero Torecillas (station NF024) had elevated concentrations of mercury in fish; arsenic in water; copper in fish, sediment, and water; and total DDT in fish and water. Puerto Morazàn (station NF017) has elevated concentrations of mercury in fish; arsenic in water; and elevated copper in sediment and water. Concentrations of copper in water in these areas may be toxic to aquatic life.

Other studies have also detected DDT in the Gulf of Fonseca. During the initial phase of the International Mussel Watch Program, DDT was detected in mussels from Isla de Aserradores (199 ppb dw) in 1991 (IMWC 1995).

Based on limited data, the Estero Padre Ramos may serve as an appropriate reference area for the Estero Real. At station NP004, total DDT was very low in water and sediment, and mercury concentrations were low in sediment. At stations NP002 and NP003, total DDT concentrations were low in water.

4.0 Conclusions and Recommendations

Contaminants, especially DDT and copper, were widely distributed in the Gulf of Fonseca. This section discusses potential sources of these contaminants in the Gulf of Fonseca. We recommend future monitoring to validate results and track progress toward reducing contamination, management actions that can mitigate or reduce contamination, and implications of Hurricane Mitch on contaminant loadings to the Gulf of Fonseca.

4.1 Potential contaminant sources

Potential sources of contamination in the Gulf of Fonseca include agricultural chemical use, waste disposal, the port and oil terminal at San Lorenzo, waste disposal in coastal communities or from upstream areas, mining, and chemicals used in shrimp aquaculture, including pesticides and diesel fuel. In this study, mercury, arsenic, copper, and DDT were identified as chemicals of concern. Potential sources of these contaminants in the Gulf of Fonseca are discussed below.

Atmospheric deposition of mercury is a major source to many areas (Eisler 2000a). Other major sources of mercury are mining and processing of gold, copper, or lead, and industrial waste disposal. In the past, mercury has been used in anti-fouling paint and fungicides (Eisler 2000a). In both fresh water and salt water, mercury is converted from inorganic to organic forms by bacteria through the process of methylation. The organic form of mercury is much more toxic than inorganic forms. Methylation is usually greatest at the sediment-water interface, but also occurs in the water column (Beckvar et al. 1996). Methylation is influenced by the availability of inorganic mercury, presence of sulfate and sulfide, oxygen, pH, salinity, organic carbon, and presence of other complexing agents. High sulfate sediments would be more suitable for methylation, since sulfate-reducing bacteria are the primary methylators of mercury, while high sulfide concentrations would inhibit methylation. High nutrient concentrations enhance methylation and high salinity inhibits methylation. Methylation also increases during summer when biological productivity and temperature are high. The concentration of total mercury in the environment is generally not a good predictor of methyl mercury availability (Beckvar et al. 1996).

Arsenic is widely used in production of agricultural chemicals, including insecticides, herbicides, fungicides, algicides, and growth stimulants (Eisler 2000b). Wood preservatives are also a major use of arsenic. The smelting and refining of ores and coal-fired power plants can also be a source of arsenic. Arsenic pesticides have been used extensively on cotton crops and as feed additives for chickens (Eisler 2000a).

Major copper sources include mining, industrial discharges, anti-fouling paints, wood-treating chemicals, fungicides, and copper-containing fertilizers (Eisler 2000a). Copper sulfate is used in agriculture as a fungicide, algicide, nutritional supplement, insecticide, and as a repellent. It is also used in water treatment to control algae. Copper sulfate used to control algae in surface waters can be toxic to resident fish and crustaceans (Eisler 2000a). Copper sulfate is used on cashews, bananas, and other crops. Cashews are grown upstream of El Tamarindo in El Salvador, where elevated concentrations of copper were detected in sediment. Rio Nacaome, Bahía Chismuyo, and the Estero Real are downstream of mining areas.

Historically heavy use of DDT as an agricultural chemical, particularly on cotton fields, most likely explains the widespread presence of DDT throughout the Gulf of Fonseca. For example, the area in El Salvador upstream of Bahía La Unión was formerly a cotton-producing area; elevated concentrations of DDT were detected in fish at La Unión. In Nicaragua, cotton was historically grown south of the Estero Real and along the Pacific coast, where elevated concentrations of DDT were detected. The widespread use of DDT has been replaced with organophosphates and carbamates (Murty 1986).

4.2   Recommended future monitoring

4.2.1   El Salvador
In El Salvador, we recommend two areas for future monitoring. At La Unión (station 57), it would be beneficial to monitor copper and DDT in fish, sediment, and water. In Estero El Tamarindo, mercury, copper, arsenic, and DDT should be analyzed in fish and water. The Rio Nacaome (stations HF047 and HF048) would be a suitable reference area for comparison.

Water samples should be collected and analyzed at least once per year (particularly at the beginning of the rainy season), while fish and sediment should be analyzed once every two to five years at the end of the dry season. Analysis should include standard reference materials for fish and sediment. We suggest additional training for the FUSADES laboratory to improve capabilities for analysis of arsenic in fish tissue and mercury in sediment.

4.2.2 Honduras
In Honduras, there are three areas that we recommend for future monitoring. At San Lorenzo (station HF046), it would be beneficial to monitor DDT in fish, sediment, and water. In Estero El Pedregal, copper, arsenic, and DDT should be sampled in fish and water. In Estero San Bernardo, DDT, copper in fish and water should be sampled. The Rio Nacaome (stations HF047 and HF048) would be a suitable reference area for comparison.

Water samples should be collected and analyzed at least once per year (particularly at the beginning of the rainy season), while fish and sediment should be analyzed once every two to five years at the end of the dry season. Analysis should include standard reference materials for fish and sediment. We suggest additional training for the CESCCO laboratory to improve capabilities for analysis of pesticides and metals in fish tissue. Developing additional capabilities for analysis of pesticides and trace elements in water (for example, by the laboratory in La Lujosa) would also be useful for shrimp aquaculture managers.

4.2.3 Nicaragua
In Nicaragua, there are two areas that we recommend for future monitoring. In Estero Torecillas (station NF024), it would be beneficial to monitor DDT, copper, and mercury in fish, sediment, and water. At Puerto Morazàn (station NF017), DDT, copper, and mercury in fish and water should be sampled. It would also be useful to sample other stations in the Estero Real. The Estero Padre Ramos (stations NP004, NP003, and NP002) would be a suitable reference area for comparison.

Water samples should be collected and analyzed at least once per year (particularly at the beginning of the rainy season), while fish and sediment should be analyzed once every two to five years at the end of the dry season. Analysis should include standard reference materials for fish and sediment. We suggest additional training for the MAGFOR laboratory to improve capabilities for analysis of DDT and metals in sediment and fish tissue.

4.3 Recommended Management Actions

If our assumptions regarding the sources of contaminants are correct, it would be expected that DDT concentrations in water, sediment, and biota would gradually decline over time as contaminated soil or sediment is eroded, buried, and redistributed. However, if the major source of copper to the Gulf of Fonseca system were the ongoing use of agricultural chemicals such as copper sulfate, concentrations of copper would not be expected to decrease as long as the chemicals are in use. Management actions that could mitigate or minimize the effects of these releases include actions that control suspended sediments or stabilize soil (for example, stabilizing or planting riparian vegetation). Reducing the use of agricultural chemicals that contain copper or arsenic would also benefit water quality. Because concentrations of DDT and copper are elevated in shrimp aquaculture areas, it would be beneficial to limit water intake into shrimp-growing ponds, at least at the beginning of the rainy season. The use of intensive aquaculture techniques would help prevent toxicity to shrimp from poor water quality.

If further sampling verifies the mercury concentrations in fish from El Tamarindo found in this study, the local community should receive information on reducing risks of mercury consumption (see appendix).

4.4   Implications of Hurricane Mitch

Hurricane Mitch temporarily re-routed the Rio Choluteca. Instead of discharging to the south of Choluteca, the river entered the Gulf of Fonseca to the west near San Lorenzo, Honduras. Based on the results of sampling and analysis it appears that the major result of Hurricane Mitch was to deposit trace elements in the area of the temporary discharge zone. Arsenic and copper are accumulating in crab and fish at stations HF042, HF043, or HF044. Copper is accumulating in fish from station HF044, and copper concentrations are elevated in surface water at stations HF041, HF042, and HF043.

5.0 References

Barraza, J.E. and A. Carballeira. 1998. Una nota corta sobre los metales pesados de la bahía de La Unión, Golfo de Fonseca, El Salvador. Publicación Ocasional No. 1. San Salvador: Ministerio de Medio Ambiente y Recursos Naturales.

Beckvar, N., J. Field, S. Salazar, and R. Hoff. 1996. Contaminants in aquatic habitats at hazardous waste sites: Mercury. NOAA Technical Memorandum NOS ORCA 100. Seattle: . Office of Ocean Resources Conservation and Assessment, National Oceanic and Atmospheric Administration. 64 pp.

Beckvar, N., Office of Response and Restoration, National Oceanic and Atmospheric Administration, Seattle, personal communication on DDT effects concentrations, May 29, 2002.

Cox, C., T.W.Clarkson, and D.E. Marsh. 1989. Dose response analysis of infants prenatally exposed to methyl mercury: an application of a single compartment model to single-strand hair analysis. *Environmental Research 49*:318-332.

Eisler,R.. 2000a. *Handbook of Chemical Risk Assessment, Health Hazards to Humans, Plants, Animals. Volume 1: Metals.* Boca Raton, Florida: Lewis Publishers.

Eisler, R. 2000b. *Handbook of Chemical Risk Assessment, Health Hazards to Humans, Plants, Animals. Volume 3: Metalloids, radiation, cumulative index to chemicals and species.* Boca Raton, Florida: Lewis Publishers.

Hatch, W.R. and W.L. Ott. 1968. Determination of Sub-microgram quantities of mercury in solution by a flameless atomic absorption technique. *Analytical Chemistry 40*:2085-2087

International Mussel Watch Committee (IMWC). 1995. International Mussel Watch Project - Initial implementation phase final report. NOAA Technical Memorandum NOS ORCA 95. Silver Spring, Maryland: Office of Ocean Resources Conversation and Assessment, National Oceanic and Atmospheric Administration. 63 pp + six Appendices

Long, E.R. and D.D. MacDonald. 1998. Recommended uses of empirically derived, sediment quality guidelines for marine and estuarine ecosystems. *Human and Ecological Risk Assessment 4*:1019-1039

MacLeod, W.D. Jr., D.W. Brown, A.J. Friedman, D.G. Burrows, O. Maynes, R.W. Pearce, C.A. Wigren, and R.G. Bogar. 1985. Standard Analytical Procedures of the NOAA National Analytical Facility, 1985-1986. Extractable Toxic Organic Compounds (2nd ed.). NOAA Technical Memorandum NMFS/NWC-92. Seattle: National Marine Fisheries Service Northwest Center.121 pp.

Marsh, D.O., G.J. Myers, T.W. Clarkson, L. Amin-Zaki, S. Tikrit, M.A. Majeed, and A.R. Dabbagh. 1981. Dose-response relationship for human fetal exposure to methyl mercury. *Clinical Toxicology 10*:1311-1318.

Matta. M.B., J. Linse, C. Cairncross. L. Francendese. and R.M. Kocan. 2001. Reproductive and transgenerational effects of methylmercury or Aroclor 1268 on *Fundulus heteroclitus*. *Environmental Toxicology and Chemistry 20*:327-335.

Murty, A.S. 1986. *Toxicity of Pesticides to Fish. Volume 1.* Boca Raton. Florida: CRC Press. 178 pp.

Sericano, J.L., E.L. Atlas, T.L. Wade, and J.M. Brooks. 1990. NOAA`s Status and Trends Mussel Watch Program: Chlorinated pesticides and PCBs in oysters (*Crassostrea virginica*) and sediments from the Gulf of Mexico, 1986-1987. *Marine Environmental Research 29*:161-203.

USEPA. 1980. Interim Method for the Sampling and Analysis of Priority Pollutants in Sediments and Fish Tissue. USEPA Contract Laboratory Program Statement of Work for Inorganic Analysis. Document Number ILM01.0. Cincinnati: U.S. Environmental Protection Agency Environmental Monitoring and Support Laboratory.

USEPA. 1995. Quality Criteria for Water. *Federal Register 60*(86):22229-22237, May 4, 1995. Washington, D.C.: U.S. Environmental Protection Agency Health and Ecological Criteria Division.

USEPA. 1997. *Mercury Study Report to Congress. Volume VII.* Characterization of human health and wildlife risks from mercury exposure in the United States. EPA-452/R97009. Washington, D.C.: U.S. Environmental Protection Agency.

USEPA. 1998. Quality Criteria for Water. *Federal Register 63*(237):68353-68364, December 10, 1998. Washington, D.C.: U.S. Environmental Protection Agency Health and Ecological Criteria Division.

USFDA. 2000. Act ion levels for poisonous or deleterious substances in human food and animal feed industry activities staff booklet. August 2000 Industry Activities Staff (HFS-565). Washington, D.C.: U.S. Food and Drug Administration. http://www.cfsan.fda.gov/~lrd/fdaact.html

Wade, T.L., E.L. Atlas, J.M. Brooks, M.C. Kennicutt II. R.G. Fox, J.L. Sericano, B. Garcia-Romero, and D. DeFreitas. 1988. NOAA Gulf of Mexico Status and Trends Program: Trace organic contaminant distribution in sediment and oysters. *Estuaries 11*:171-179.

Appendix: Health Guidance on Mercury Consumption

Information on the health effects of mercury and how to minimize them can be found at the following websites:

http://www.epa.gov/waterscience/fishadvice/advice.html

http://www.epa.gov/waterscience/fish/brochure.html

http://www.floridaconservation.org/fishing/health.html

http://www.state.nj.us/dep/dsr/bass-pickerel.htm

United States Environmental Protection Agency
Office of Water 4301
EPA-823-F-01-004
January 2001

National Advice on Mercury in Fish Caught by Family and Friends: For Women Who Are Pregnant or May Become Pregnant, Nursing Mothers, and Young Children

Summary
EPA is issuing a national advisory concerning risks associated with mercury in freshwater fish caught by friends and family. The groups most vulnerable to the effects of mercury pollution include: women who are pregnant or may become pregnant, nursing mothers, and young children. To protect against the risks of mercury in fish caught in freshwaters, EPA is recommending that these groups limit fish consumption to one meal per week for adults (6 ounces of cooked fish, 8 ounces uncooked fish) and one meal per week for young children (2 ounces cooked fish or 3 ounces uncooked fish).

Background
Mercury is a naturally occurring element that is present throughout the environment and in plants and animals. Most mercury pollution is released into the air and then falls directly onto waterways or is deposited onto land where it can be washed into the water. Mercury concentrations in air are usually low and of little direct concern. But when mercury enters the water, biological processes transform it into a highly toxic form - methylmercury. Methylmercury accumulates in fish, with larger fish generally accumulating higher levels of methylmercury.

Freshwater fish from contaminated waters have been shown to have particularly high levels of methylmercury, posing potential risks for recreational anglers and people who regularly fish for food. A recent report by the National Academy of Sciences (NAS, Toxicological Effects of Methylmercury, July 2000) confirms that methylmercury is a potent toxin and concludes that the babies of women who consume large amounts of fish when pregnant are at greater risk for changes in their nervous system that can affect their ability to learn. EPA and the states are working to reduce mercury pollution in the environment, but because methylmercury is very persistent, it will be many years before methylmercury levels in fish and the environment are reduced.

Is it safe to eat fish?
Fish is an excellent source of nutrition and most people have no reason to limit their fish consumption. Because the developing nervous system of a baby and young child is more sensitive to methylmercury's harmful effects than the more fully developed nervous system of an older child or adult, EPA is recommending that women who are pregnant or may become pregnant, nursing mothers, and young children limit their consumption of fish caught by family and friends to one meal per week (six ounces cooked fish or eight ounces uncooked fish per adult; two ounces cooked fish or three ounces uncooked fish per young child). Other family members do not need to follow this advice, but should follow recommendations of their state or local health department on the amount of fish caught by friends and family that is safe to eat.

Why is EPA issuing national fish consumption advice?
EPA is issuing this advice for women who are pregnant or may become pregnant, nursing mothers, and young children to raise awareness of the potential harm that high levels of methylmercury in fish can cause to a baby or child's developing brain and nervous system. This advice provides guidance on the amount of fish caught by friends and family that these groups can eat to keep methylmercury from reaching harmful levels.

EPA's fish advisory web site: www.epa.gov/ost/fish/ or contact Jeff Bigler at bigler.jeff@epa.gov.

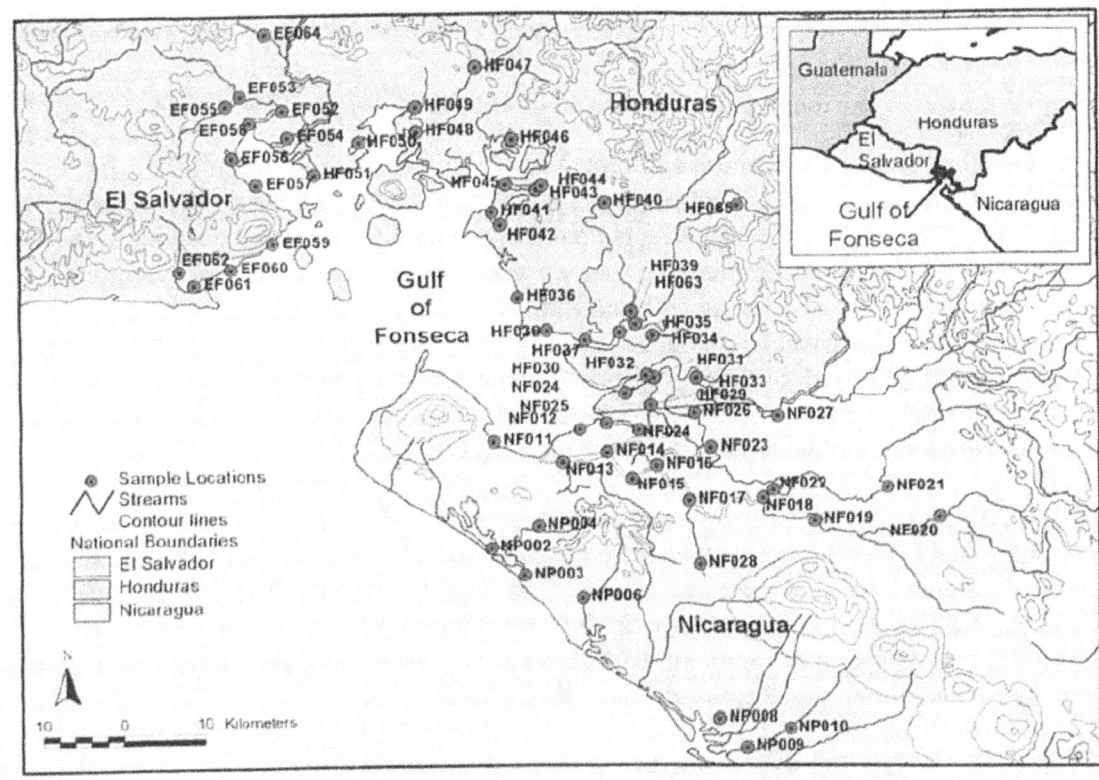

Figure 1. Station location.

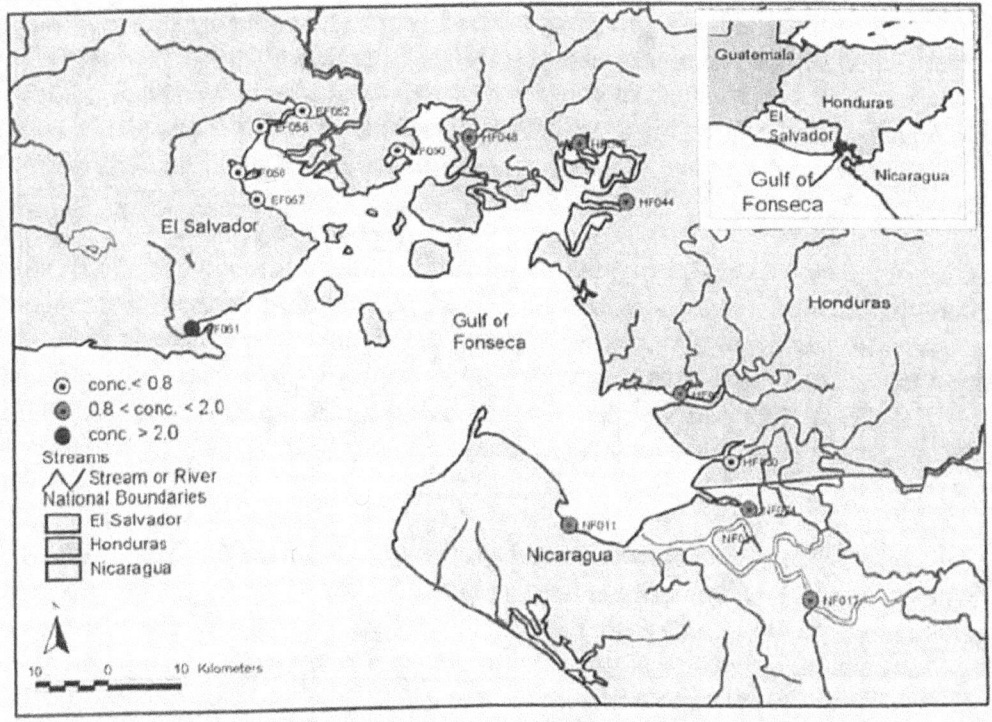

Figure 2. Mercury (ppm dw) in fish muscle (as reported by NI, ES, and GE labs).

23

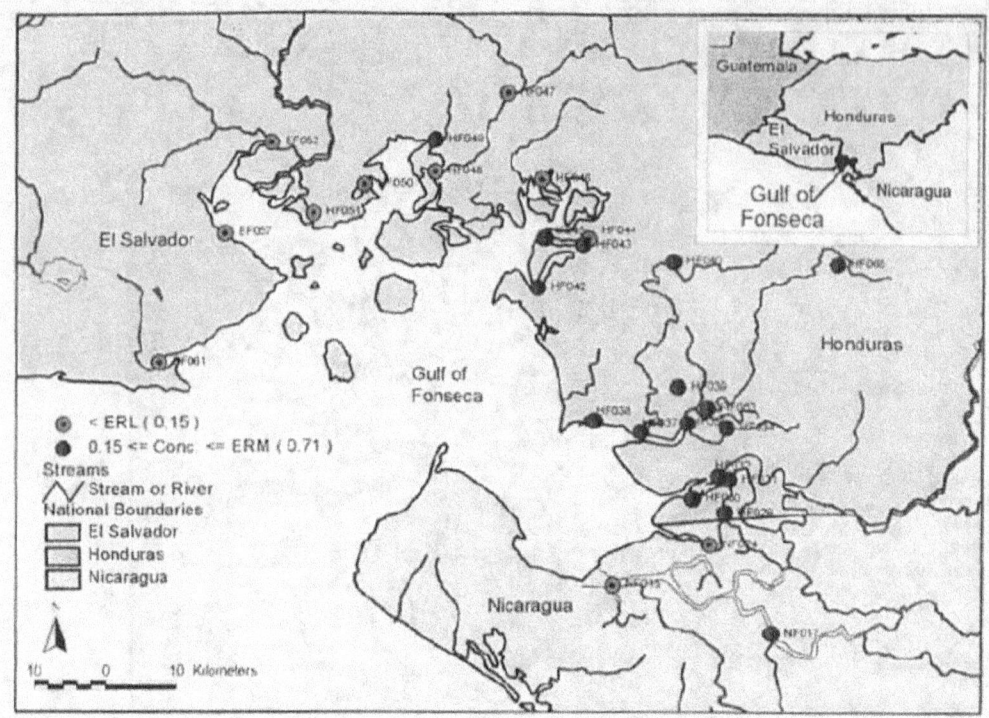

Figure 3. Mercury (ppm dw) in sediment (as reported by GE lab).

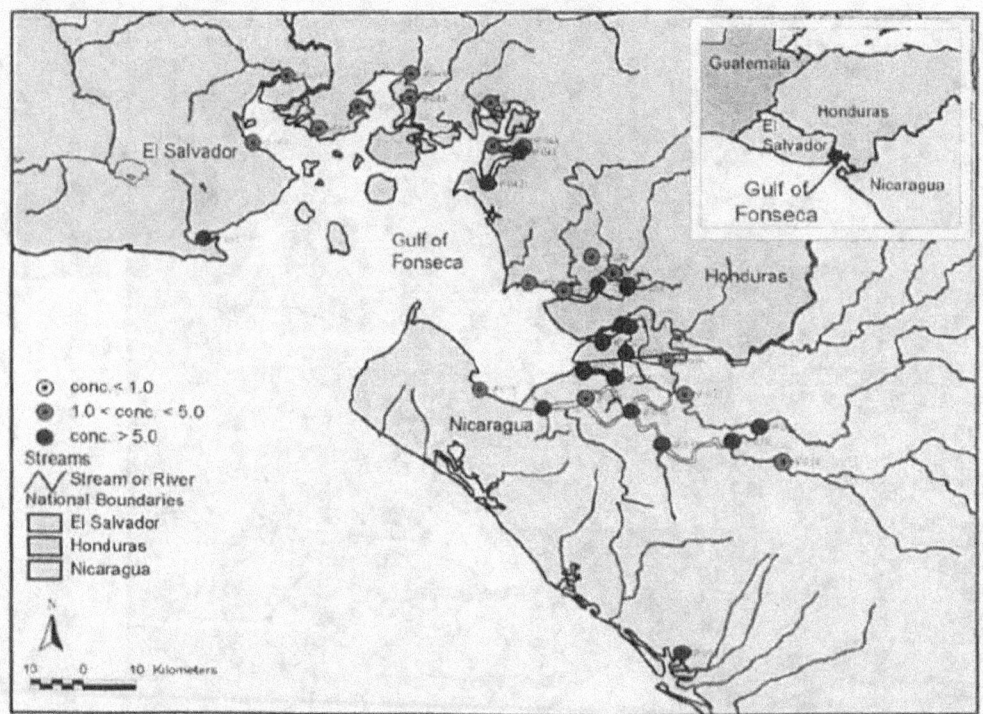

Figure 4. Arsenic (ppm dw) in whole fiddler crab (as reported by NI and GE labs).

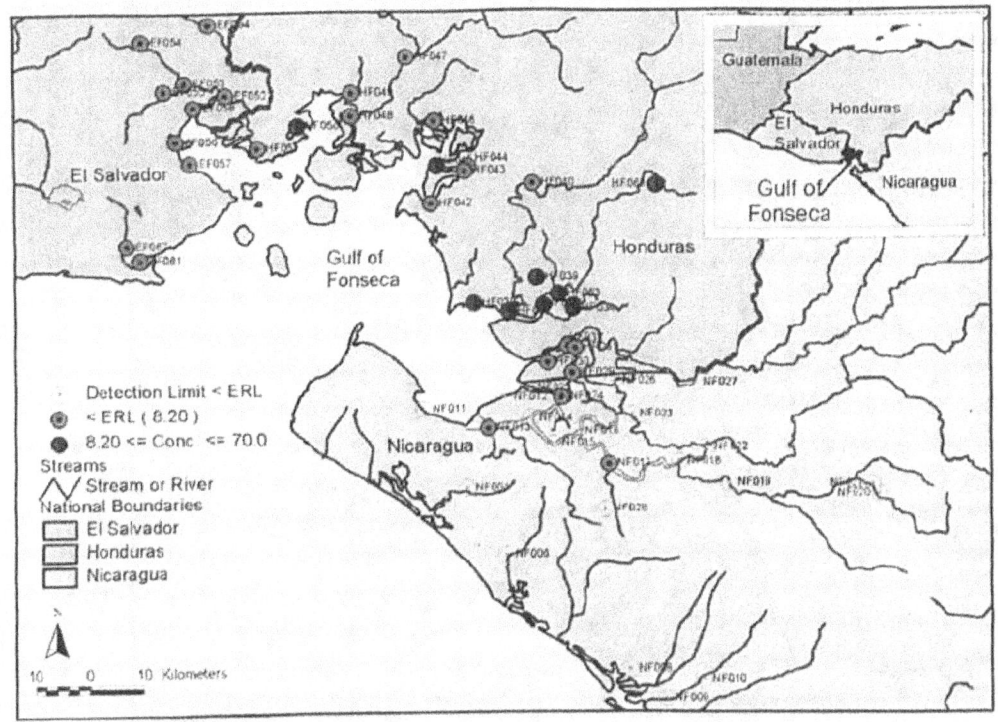

Figure 5. Arsenic (ppm dw) in sediment (as reported by all labs).

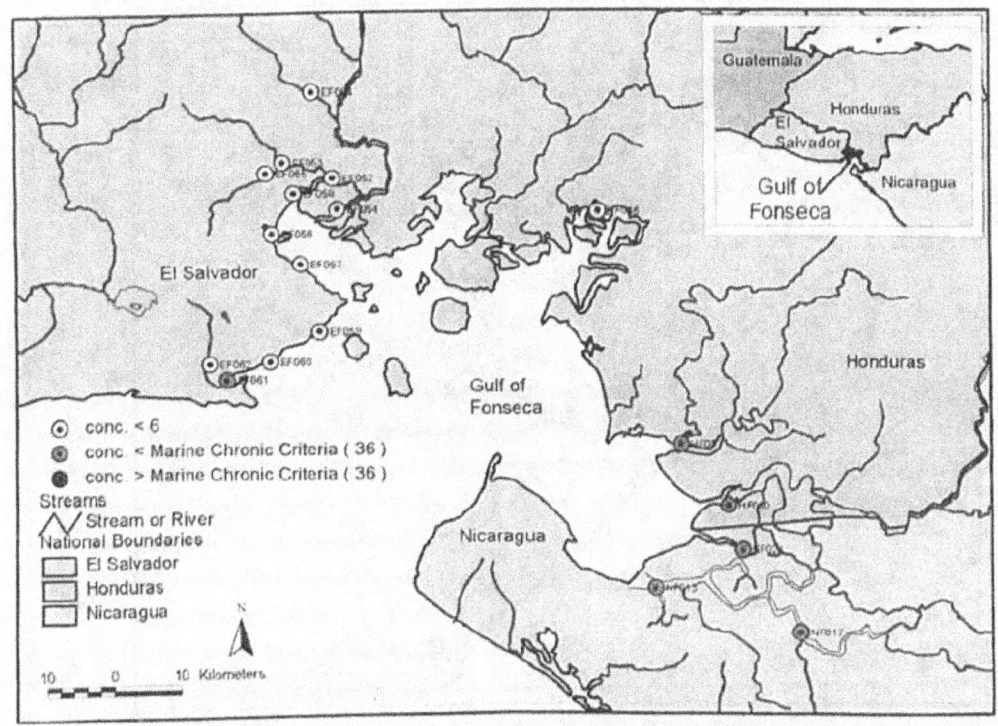

Figure 6. Arsenic (ppb) in unfiltered surface water (as reported by ES, HO, and GE labs).

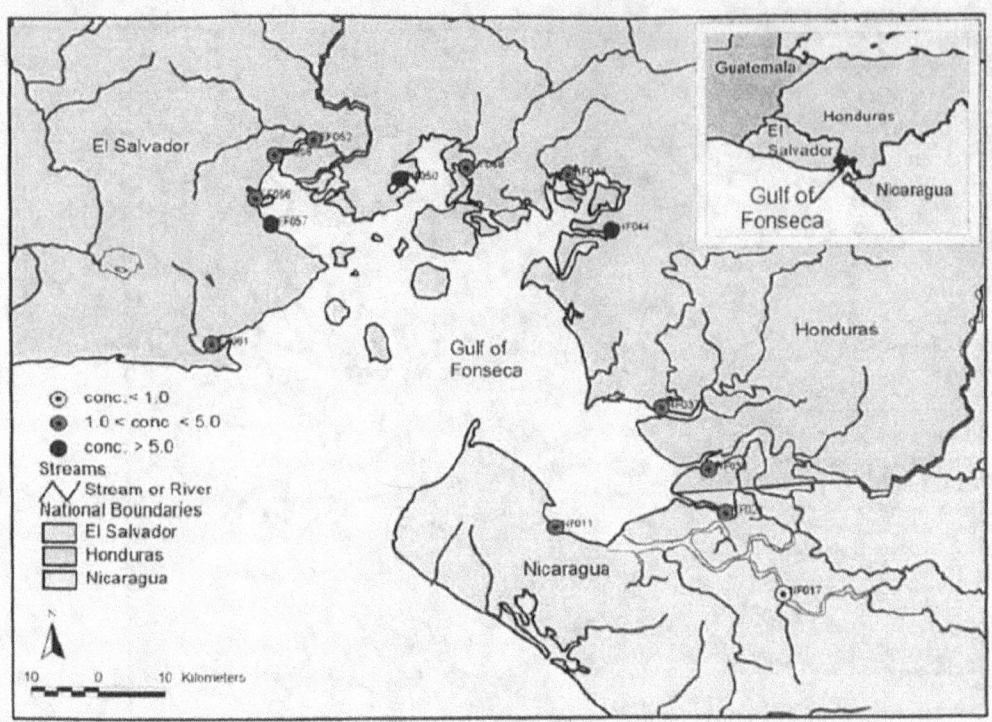

Figure 7. Copper (ppm dw) in fish muscle (as reported by ES and GE labs).

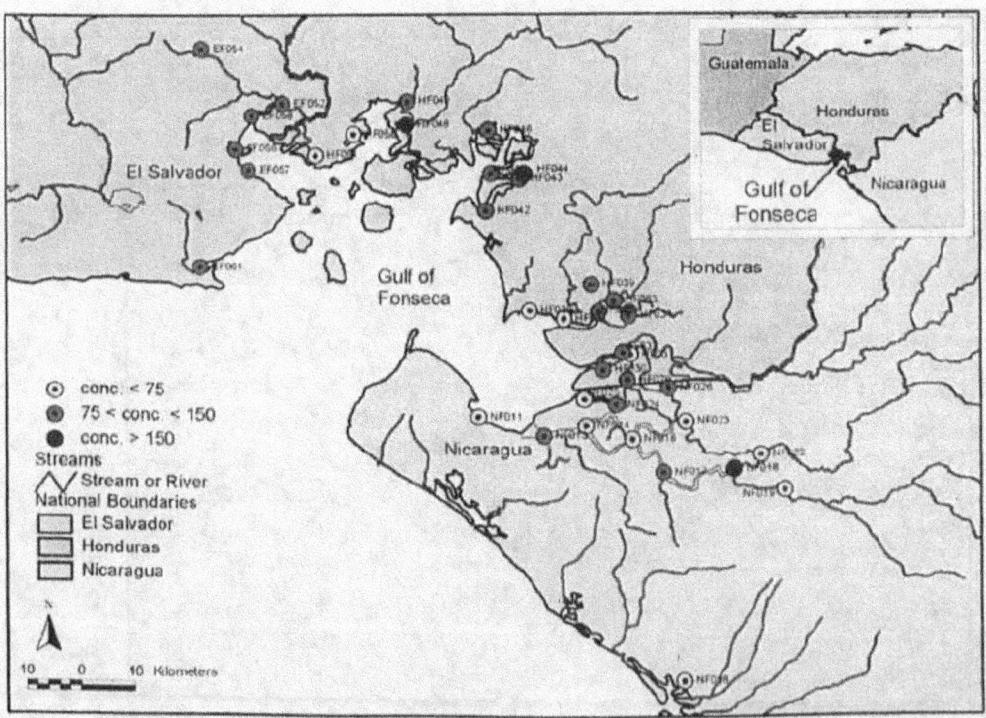

Figure 8. Copper (ppm dw) in whole fiddler crab (as reported by NI, ES, and GE labs).

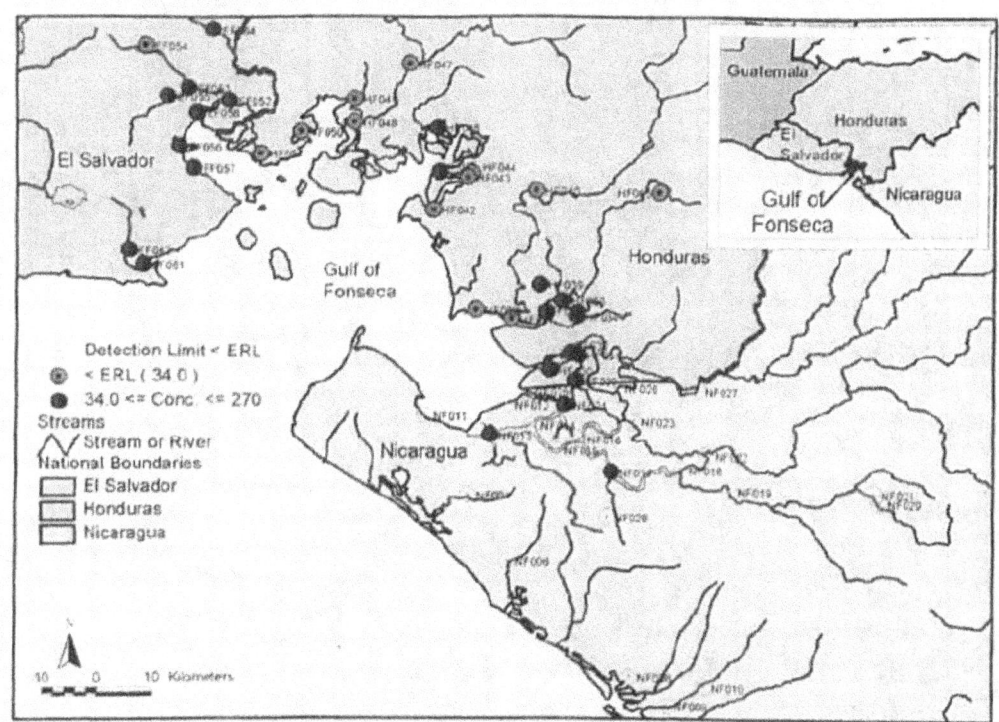

Figure 9. Copper (ppm dw) in sediment (as reported by all labs).

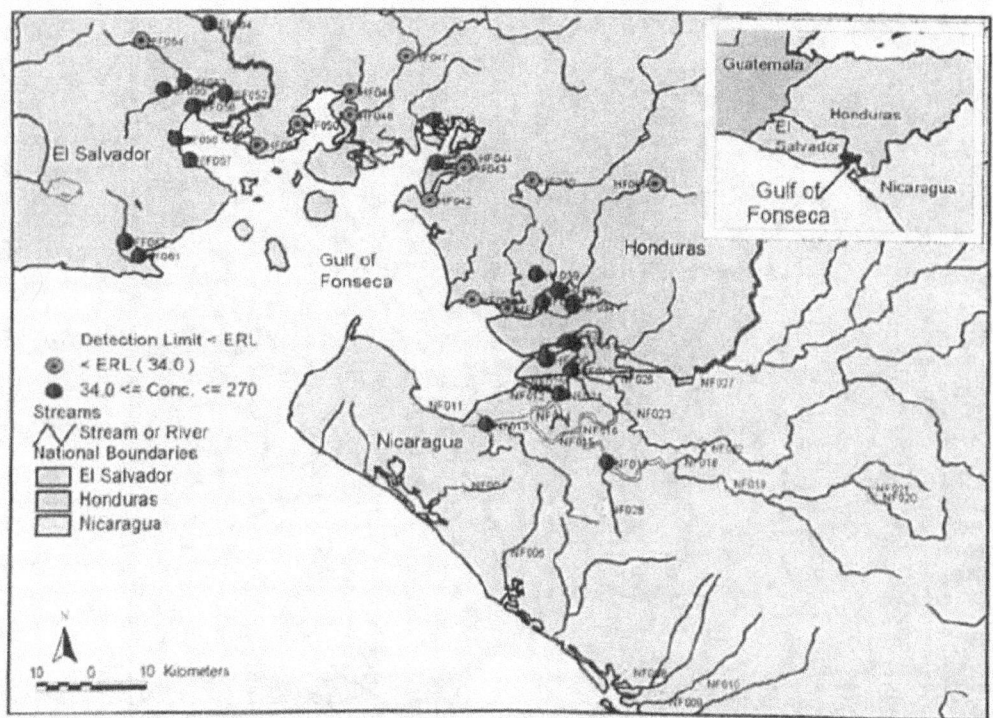

Figure 10. Copper (ppb) in unfiltered surface water (as reported by ES, HO, and GE labs).

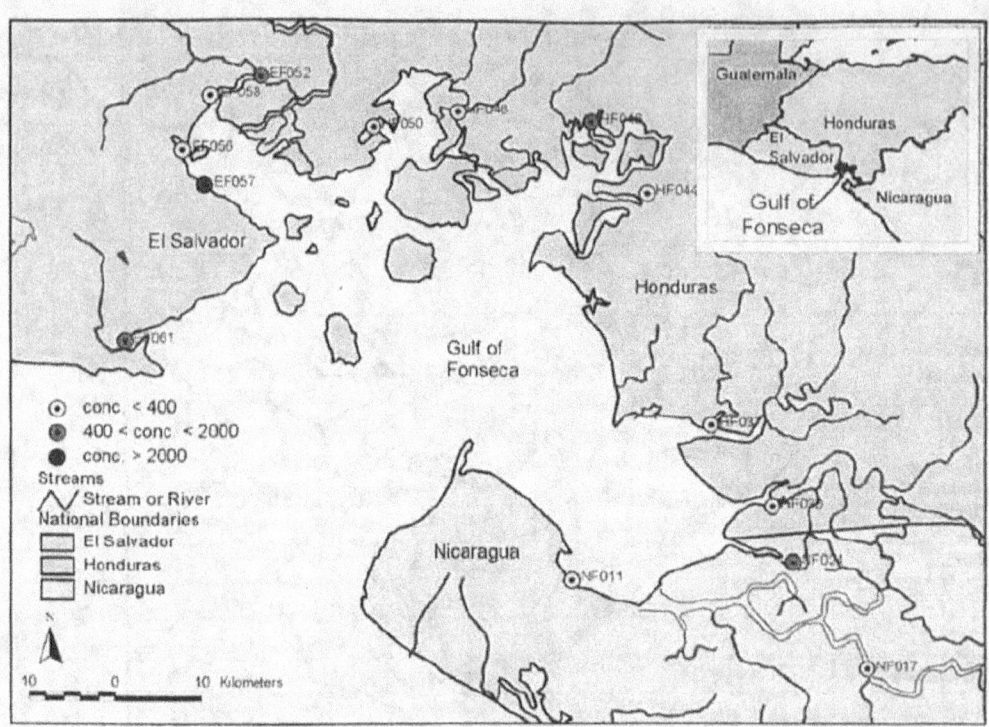

Figure 11. Total DDT (ppb dw) in fish muscle (as reported by NI, ES, GE labs).

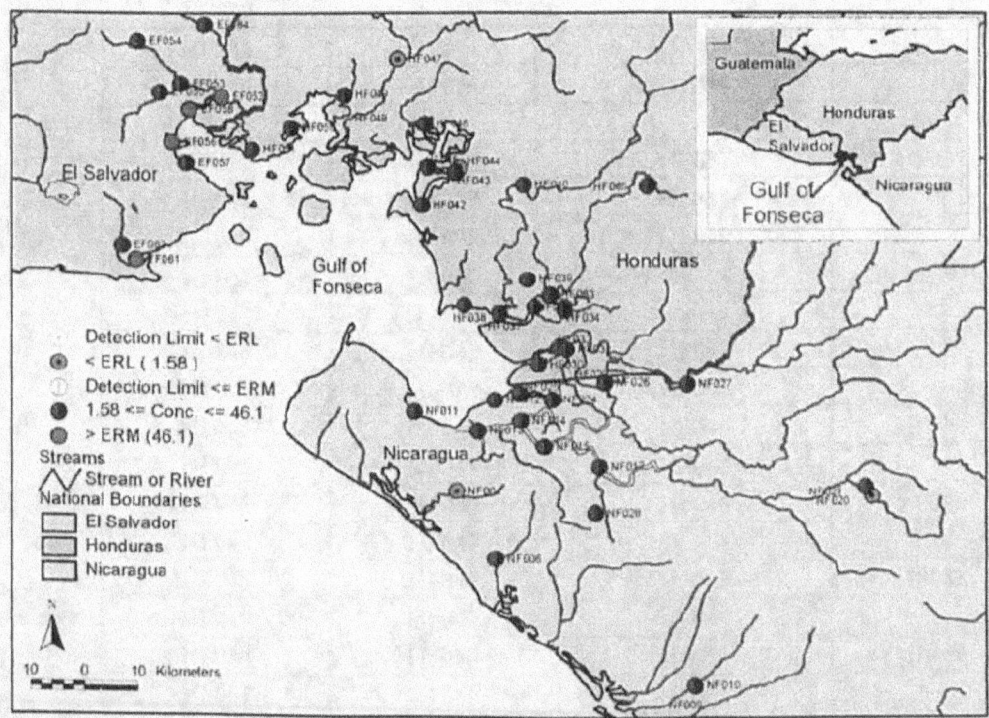

Figure 12. Total DDT (ppb dw) in sediment (as reported by NI, ES, and GE labs).

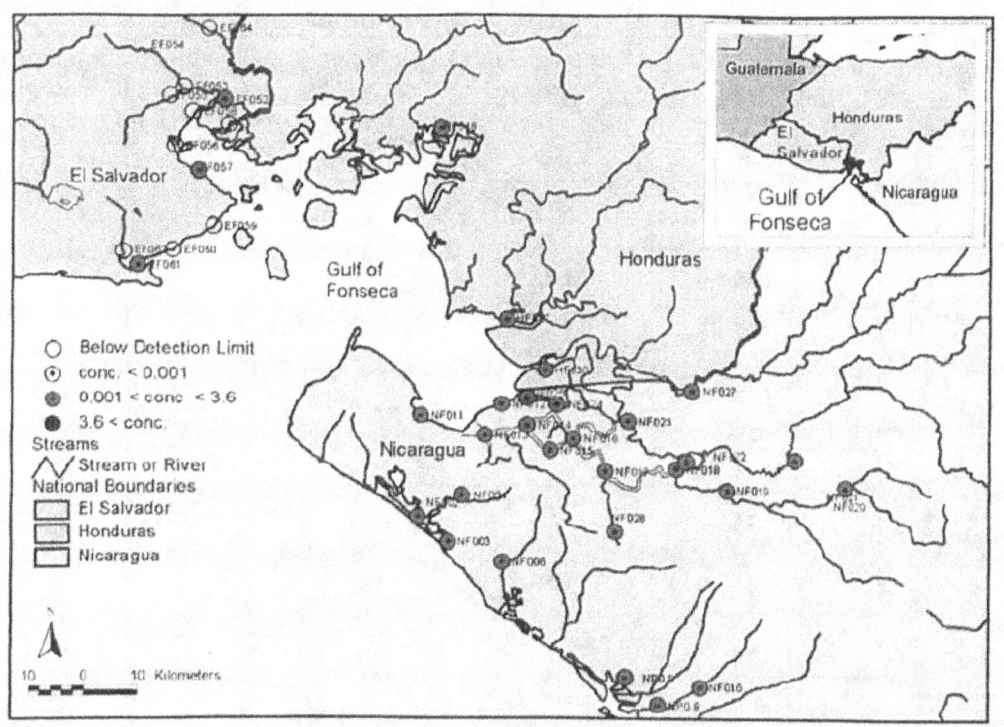

Figure 13. Total DDT (ppb) in unfiltered surface water (as reported by NI, ES, and GE labs).

Table 1. Water, sediment, fiddler crab, and fish sample locations.

Country	Water Sample Stations	Sediment Sample Stations	Fiddler Crab Sample Stations	Fish Sample Stations
El Salvador				
	EF052	EF052	EF052	EF052
	EF053	EF053		
	EF054	EF054	EF054	
	EF055	EF055		
	EF056	EF056	EF056	EF056
	EF057	EF057	EF057	EF057
	EF058	EF058	EF058	EF058
	EF059			
	EF060			
	EF061	EF061	EF061	EF061
	EF062	EF062		
	EF064	EF064		
Honduras				
	HF029	HF029	HF029	
	HF030	HF030	HF030	HF030
	HF031	HF031	HF031	
	HF032	HF032	HF032	
	HF033			
	HF034	HF034	HF034	
	HF035	HF035	HF035	
	HF036			
	HF037	HF037	HF037	HF037
	HF038	HF038	HF038	
	HF039	HF039	HF039	
	HF040	HF040		
	HF041			
	HF042	HF042	HF042	
	HF043	HF043	HF043	
	HF044	HF044	HF044	HF044
	HF045	HF045	HF045	
	HF046	HF046	HF046	HF046
	HF047	HF047		
	HF048	HF048	HF048	HF048
	HF049	HF049	HF049	
	HF050	HF050	HF050	HF050
	HF051	HF051	HF051	
	HF063	HF063	HF063	
		HF065		

Table 1. Water, sediment, fiddler crab, and fish sample locations, cont.

Country	Water Sample Stations	Sediment Sample Stations	Fiddler Crab Sample Stations	Fish Sample Stations
Nicaragua				
	NP002			
	NP003			
	NP004	NP004		
	NP006	NP006		
	NP008	NP008	NP008	
	NP009	NP009		
	NP010	NP010		
	NF011	NF011	NF011	NF011
	NF012	NF012		
	NF013	NF013	NF013	
	NF014	NF014	NF014	
	NF015	NF015		
	NF016	NF016	NF016	
	NF017	NF017	NF017	NF017
	NF018	NF018	NF018	
	NF019	NF019	NF019	
	NF020	NF020		
	NF021	NF021		
	NF022	NF022	NF022	
	NF023	NF023	NF023	
	NF024	NF024	NF024	NF024
	NF025	NF025	NF025	
	NF026	NF026	NF026	
	NF027	NF027	NF027	
	NF028	NF028		

Table 2. Water screening concentrations (ambient water quality criteria).

Contaminant	Chronic AWQC ppb	Acute AWQC ppb
Mercury	0.025	2
Arsenic	36	69
Copper	3.1	13
DDT	0.005	3.6
malathion	0.1	
parathion	0.013	0.065

Table 3. Sediment screening concentrations.

Contaminant	ER-L	ER-M
Mercury (ppm)	0.15	0.71
Arsenic (ppm)	8.2	70
Copper (ppm)	34	270
DDT (ppb)	1.58	46.1
PAHs (ppb)	4022	44792

Table 4. Analysis of standard reference materials--questionable results.

	GERG	FUSADES	MAGFOR	CESCCO
Sediment				
Organochlorines	acceptable	acceptable	alpha chlordane gamma chlordane 2,4'DDE 2,4'DDD	N.R.
Trace elements	selenium	acceptable	arsenic selenium mercury	N.R.
Tissue				
Organochlorines	acceptable	acceptable	2,4' DDE 4,4' DDE 2,4' DDD 4,4' DDD 2,4' DDT 4,4' DDT alpha chlordane dieldrin	N.R.
Trace elements	lead nickel	arsenic	cadmium lead selenium copper nickel zinc	N.R.

N.R. not reported

Table 5. Mercury results.

Station	Lab	Water Conc. (ppb)	Qual Code	Sediment Conc. (ppm)	Qual Code	Catfish Conc. (ppm)	Qual Code	Crab Conc. (ppm)	Qual Code
EF052	ES	1.19		5.093		0.224			
EF052	GE	0.125	J	0.12	J	0.462		0.071	J
EF052	HO	N/A		0.011	U				
EF052	NI	1.25	U	0.140		0.402		0.081	
EF053	ES	4.12		10.91					
EF054	ES	1.5		6.614				0.161	
EF055	ES	8.5		1.521					
EF056	ES	1.55		2.770		0.266	J	0.226	J
EF056	GE					0.37			
EF056	NI					0.22			
EF057	ES	3.96		2.436		0.210	J	0.181	J
EF057	GE	0.162	J	0.12	J	0.213		0.068	J
EF057	HO	N/A		0.011	U				
EF057	NI	1.25	U	0.169		0.185			
EF058	ES	2.25		1.694		0.176	J	0.165	J
EF058	GE					0.489			
EF058	NI					0.4			
EF059	ES	1.31							
EF060	ES	0.98							
EF061	ES	1.5		1.818		1.834	J	0.237	J
EF061	GE	0.169	J	0.12	J	6.621		0.061	J
EF061	HO	N/A		0.011	U				
EF061	NI	1.25	U	0.131		5.996		0.103	
EF062	ES	2.54		1.670					
EF064	ES	3		1.549					
HF029	GE			0.16	J			0.1	J
HF030	ES	15.5		2.029		0.260	J	0.275	J
HF030	GE	0.193	J	0.17	J	0.467		0.081	J
HF030	HO	N/A		0.011	U				
HF030	NI	1.25	U	0.218		0.418		0.192	
HF031	GE			0.16	J			0.094	J
HF032	GE			0.17	J			0.09	J
HF034	GE			0.21				0.086	J
HF035	ES							0.213	J
HF035	GE			0.22				0.087	J
HF035	NI							0.186	
HF037	ES	2.5		1.849		0.230	J	0.241	J
HF037	GE	0.352	J	0.21		0.782		0.092	J

Table 5. Mercury results, cont.

Station	Lab	Water Conc. (ppb)	Qual Code	Sediment Conc. (ppm)	Qual Code	Catfish Conc. (ppm)	Qual Code	Crab Conc. (ppm)	Qual Code
HF037	HO	N/A		0.011	U				
HF037	NI	1.25	U	0.144		1.37		0.232	
HF038	GE			0.19				0.092	J
HF039	GE			0.26				0.1	J
HF040	GE			0.17	J				
HF042	GE			0.16	J			0.125	J
HF043	GE			0.23				0.157	J
HF044	GE			0.13	J	1.038		0.106	J
HF045	GE			0.23				0.102	J
HF046	ES	3.27		2.22		0.300	J		
HF046	GE	0.167	J	0.14	J	0.851		0.083	J
HF046	HO	N/A		0.011	U				
HF046	NI	1.25	U	0.108		0.286			
HF047	GE			0.07	J				
HF048	GE			0.08	J	0.848		0.092	J
HF049	GE			0.16	J			0.089	J
HF050	GE			0.13	J	0.232		0.078	J
HF051	GE			0.12	J			0.078	J
HF063	GE			0.22				0.126	J
HF065	GE			0.19	J				
NF011	GE					0.943			
NF011	NI	1.25	U	0.155		1.5		0.186	
NF012	NI	1.25	U	0.152					
NF013	ES	1		1.645					
NF013	GE	0.184	J	0.14	J			0.087	J
NF013	HO	N/A		0.011	U				
NF013	NI	1.25	U	0.195				0.146	
NF014	NI	1.25	U	0.148				0.168	
NF015	NI	1.25	U	0.126					
NF016	NI	1.25	U	0.147				0.14	
NF017	ES	3.5		1.800		0.291	J		
NF017	GE	0.194	J	0.15	J	0.961		0.064	J
NF017	NI	1.25	U	0.093		1.408		0.152	
NF018	NI	1.25	U	0.286				0.162	
NF019	NI	1.25	U	0.228				0.156	
NF020	NI	1.25	U	0.093					
NF021	NI	1.25	U	0.007					
NF022	NI	1.25	U	0.169				0.174	
NF023	NI	1.25	U	0.163				0.163	

Table 5. Mercury results, cont.

Station	Lab	Water Conc. (ppb)	Water Qual Code	Sediment Conc. (ppm)	Sediment Qual Code	Catfish Conc. (ppm)	Catfish Qual Code	Crab Conc. (ppm)	Crab Qual Code
NF024	ES	1		1.523					
NF024	GE	0.165	J	0.13	J	0.791		0.081	J
NF024	HO	N/A		0.011	U				
NF024	NI	1.25	U	0.151		1.26		0.16	
NF025	NI	1.25	U	0.134				0.179	
NF026	NI	1.25	U	0.161				0.171	
NF027	NI	1.25	U	0.013					
NF028	NI	1.25	U	0.007					

J - estimated concentration
U - below detection limit (concentration is detection limit)
ES - FUSADES
GE - Texas A&M
HO - CESCCO
NI - MAGFOR
N/A - not analyzed

Table 6. Arsenic results.

Station	Lab	Water Conc. (ppb)	Water Qual. Code	Sediment Conc. (ppm)	Sediment Qual. Code	Catfish Conc. (ppm)	Catfish Qual. Code	Crab Conc. (ppm)	Crab Qual. Code
EF052	ES	0.54		0.138		0.184		0.627	J
EF052	GE	2.02	J	6.36		1.932		2.908	
EF052	HO	N/A		1.535	U				
EF052	NI	5	U	0.077	U	2.161		2.406	
EF053	ES	0.06		0.066					
EF054	ES	0.34		0.615				0.235	J
EF055	ES	0.51		0.057					
EF056	ES	0.55		0.254		0.257	J	0.557	J
EF056	GE					1.694			
EF056	NI					0.904			
EF057	ES	0.42		0.086		0.166	J	0.604	J
EF057	GE	2.434	J	5.33		3.394		2.254	
EF057	HO	N/A		1.535	U				
EF057	NI	5	U	0.077	U	2.324			
EF058	ES	0.55		0.123		0.183	J	0.639	J
EF058	GE					2.786			
EF058	NI					3.892			
EF059	ES	0.41							
EF060	ES	0.35							
EF061	ES	0.37		0.089		0.340	J	0.338	J
EF061	GE	7.26		6.18		45.141		3.004	
EF061	HO	N/A		1.535	U				
EF061	NI	5	U	0.077	U	13.247		9.031	
EF062	ES	0.16		0.058					
EF064	ES	0.63		0.129					
HF029	GE			6.12				5.516	
HF030	ES	1.02		0.103		0.178	J	0.264	J
HF030	GE	6.45		7.58		10.973		4.293	
HF030	HO	N/A		1.535	U				
HF030	NI	5	U	0.077	U	12.146		6.181	
HF031	GE			7.32				5.282	
HF032	GE			7.09				5.212	
HF034	GE			8.7				5.24	
HF035	ES							0.278	J
HF035	GE			8.61				4.777	
HF035	NI							14.122	
HF037	ES	2.83		0.120		0.197	J	0.307	J
HF037	GE	14.411		8.43		11.75		3.365	

Table 6. Arsenic results, cont.

Station	Lab	Water Conc. (ppb)	Water Qual. Code	Sediment Conc. (ppm)	Sediment Qual. Code	Catfish Conc. (ppm)	Catfish Qual. Code	Crab Conc. (ppm)	Crab Qual. Code
HF037	HO	N/A		1.535	U				
HF037	NI	5	U	0.078		2.27		0.909	
HF038	GE			8.53				2.658	
HF039	GE			9.43				3.57	
HF040	GE			7.17					
HF042	GE			7.66				5.788	
HF043	GE			8.19				8.294	
HF044	GE			6.66		21.76		4.317	
HF045	GE			9.88				4.288	
HF046	ES	0.42		0.102		0.246	J		
HF046	GE	3.02	J	6.51		9.453		4.051	
HF046	HO	N/A		1.535	U				
HF046	NI	5	U	0.077	U	6.09			
HF047	GE			4.98					
HF048	GE			4.48		2.809		2.517	
HF049	GE			8.15				3.456	
HF050	GE			8.89		1.612		3.482	
HF051	GE			7.19				4.991	
HF063	GE			9.42				3.3	
HF065	GE			10.49					
NF011	ES					0.160	J		
NF011	GE					6.148			
NF011	NI	5	U	0.077	U	3.607		3.376	
NF012	NI	5	U	0.077	U				
NF013	ES	0.39		0.109				0.293	J
NF013	GE	7.31		7.88				2.896	
NF013	HO	N/A		1.535	U				
NF013	NI	5	U	0.077	U			8.93	
NF014	NI	5	U	0.077	U			3.086	
NF015	NI	5	U	0.077	U				
NF016	NI	5	U	0.077	U			5.21	
NF017	ES	1.31		0.143		0.154	J	0.340	J
NF017	GE	8.94		8.11		1.938		2.153	
NF017	NI	5	U	0.077	U	4.486		5.428	
NF018	NI	1		0.077	U			6.487	
NF019	NI	5	U	0.077	U			4.674	
NF020	NI	5	U	0.077	U				
NF021	NI	5	U	0.077	U				

Table 6. Arsenic results, cont.

Station	Lab	Water Conc. (ppb)	Water Qual. Code	Sediment Conc. (ppm)	Sediment Qual. Code	Catfish Conc. (ppm)	Catfish Qual. Code	Crab Conc. (ppm)	Crab Qual. Code
NF022	NI	5	U	0.077	U			7.028	
NF023	NI	5	U	0.077	U			2.658	
NF024	ES	0.52		0.104		0.18537	J	0.302	J
NF024	GE	6.87		7.78		6.947		3.083	
NF024	HO	N/A		1.535	U				
NF024	NI	5	U	0.077	U	5.702		5.816	
NF025	NI	5	U	0.077	U			7.847	
NF026	NI	5	U	0.077	U			4.999	
NF027	NI	5	U	0.077	U				
NF028	NI	5	U	0.077	U				

J - estimated concentration
U - below detection limit (concentration is detection limit)
ES - FUSADES
GE - Texas A&M
HO - CESCCO
NI - MAGFOR
N/A - not analyzed

Table 7. Copper results.

Station	Lab	Water Conc. (ppb)	Qual. Code	Sediment Conc. (ppm)	Qual. Code	Catfish Conc. (ppm)	Qual. Code	Crab Conc. (ppm)	Qual. Code
EF052	ES	2.74		56.818		1.236	J	110.695	J
EF052	GE	0.485		52.87		2.374		87.844	
EF052	HO	3	U	22.05					
EF052	NI	1000	U	0.221	U	14	U	37.01	
EF053	ES	4.33		57.78					
EF054	ES	3.53		27.321				82.051	J
EF055	ES	1.84		93.581					
EF056	ES	2.42		45.613		0.735	J	98.210	J
EF056	GE					1.879			
EF056	NI					14	U		
EF057	ES	2.69		40.743		0.776	J	94.965	J
EF057	GE	0.567		41.88		5.041		32.222	
EF057	HO	11		4.25					
EF057	NI	1000	U	0.221	U	14	U		
EF058	ES	7.79		48.795		0.125		122.566	J
EF058	GE					2.235			
EF058	NI					14	U		
EF059	ES	8.25							
EF060	ES	7.27							
EF061	ES	3.82		84.439		0.469	J	109.413	J
EF061	GE	0.578		75.78		1.848		56.433	
EF061	HO	25		21.94					
EF061	NI	1000	U	0.221	U	14	U	65.684	
EF062	ES	18.06		81.625					
EF064	ES	3.22		60.192					
HF029	GE			46.35				142.601	
HF029	HO	38							
HF030	ES	9.61		47.397		0.757	J	45.754	J
HF030	GE	1.602		45.84		2.897		109.527	
HF030	HO	174		0.59					
HF030	NI	1000	U	0.221	U	14	U	66.589	
HF031	GE			43.7				74.597	
HF031	HO	53							
HF032	GE			47.79				84.221	
HF032	HO	148							
HF033	HO	32							
HF034	GE			38.94				132.164	

Table 7. Copper results, cont.

Station	Lab	Water Conc. (ppb)	Qual. Code	Sediment Conc. (ppm)	Qual. Code	Catfish Conc. (ppm)	Qual. Code	Crab Conc. (ppm)	Qual. Code
HF034	HO	69							
HF035	ES							50.096	J
HF035	GE			37.48				81.813	
HF035	HO	54							
HF035	NI							72.455	
HF036	HO	192							
HF037	ES	15.88		31.907		0.122		62.158	J
HF037	GE	2.995		26.87		4.933		58.485	
HF037	HO	38		8.27					
HF037	NI	1000	U	0.221	U	14	U	14	U
HF038	GE			29.79				59.91	
HF038	HO	78							
HF039	GE			38.82				113.702	
HF039	HO	3	U						
HF040	GE			20.59					
HF040	HO	3	U						
HF041	HO	68							
HF042	GE			19.24				149.062	
HF042	HO	72							
HF043	GE			23.66				137.782	
HF043	HO	54							
HF044	GE			21.48		5.704		167.154	
HF044	HO	23							
HF045	GE			34.12				97.234	
HF045	HO	46							
HF046	ES	2.49		35.714		0.368	J		
HF046	GE	0.388		27.15		2.292		89.299	
HF046	HO	54		22.48					
HF046	NI	1000	U	0.221	U	14	U		
HF047	GE			20.39					
HF047	HO	3	U						
HF048	GE			9.87		2.062		155.586	
HF048	HO	3	U						
HF049	GE			31.57				109.062	
HF049	HO	3	U						
HF050	GE			33.56		20.189		67.196	
HF050	HO	2							
HF051	GE			29.97				74.63	
HF051	HO	38							

Table 7. Copper results, cont.

Station	Lab	Water Conc. (ppb)	Qual. Code	Sediment Conc. (ppm)	Qual. Code	Catfish Conc. (ppm)	Qual. Code	Crab Conc. (ppm)	Qual. Code
HF063	GE			36.21				111.824	
HF063	HO	38							
HF065	GE			25.17					
NF011	ES					0.416	J		
NF011	GE					2.323			
NF011	NI	1000	U	0.221	U	14	U	68.172	
NF012	NI	1000	U	0.221	U				
NF013	ES	3		50.935				107.056	J
NF013	GE	0.579		45.62				93.463	
NF013	HO	57		29.37					
NF013	NI	1000	U	0.221	U			95.863	.
NF014	NI	1000	U	0.221	U			14	U
NF015	NI	1000	U	0.221	U				
NF016	NI	1000	U	0.221	U			55.212	
NF017	ES	9.43		51.325		0.381	J	120.968	J
NF017	GE	1.058		45.65		0.978		101.756	
NF017	HO	9							
NF017	NI	1000	U	0.221	U	14	U	53.529	
NF018	NI	1000	U	0.221	U			167.293	
NF019	NI	1000	U	0.221	U			72.509	
NF020	NI	1000	U	0.221	U				
NF021	NI	1000	U	0.221	U				
NF022	NI	1000	U	0.221	U			57.905	
NF023	NI	1000	U	0.221	U			30.025	
NF024	ES	4.75		47.056		3.728	J	100.273	J
NF024	GE	0.377		41.53		1.564		102.89	
NF024	HO	167		10.97					
NF024	NI	1000	U	0.221	U	14	U	63.214	
NF025	NI	1000	U	0.221	U			14	U
NF026	NI	1000	U	0.221	U			90.844	
NF027	NI	1000	U	0.221	U				
NF028	NI	1000	U	0.221	U				

J - estimated concentration
U - below detection limit (concentration is detection limit)
ES - FUSADES
GE - Texas A&M
HO - CESCCO
NI - MAGFOR
N/A - not analyzed

Table 8. PAH results.

Station	Lab	Water Conc. (ppb)	Qual Code	Sediment Conc. (ppb)	Qual Code
EF052	GE	0.153		175.5	
EF057	GE	0.193		150.7	
EF061	GE	0.159		140.9	
HF029	GE			31.3	
HF030	GE	0.196		177.2	
HF031	GE			183.5	
HF032	GE			225.2	
HF034	GE			240.4	
HF035	GE			221.14	
HF037	GE	0.331		149.2	
HF038	GE			191.6	
HF039	GE			261.4	
HF040	GE			79.1	
HF042	GE			93.5	
HF043	GE			77.6	
HF044	GE			34.8	
HF045	GE			143.1	
HF046	GE	0.1742		403.8	
HF047	GE			16	
HF048	GE			11.6	
HF049	GE			99.4	
HF050	GE			168.7	
HF051	GE			106.2	
HF063	GE			269	
HF065	GE			149.8	
NF013	GE	0.081		231.3	
NF017	GE	0.122		156.9	
NF024	GE	0.131		206	

GE - Texas A&M
N/A - not analyzed

Table 9. Total DDT results.

Station	Lab	Water Conc. (ppb)	Water Qual. Code	Sediment Conc. (ppb)	Sediment Qual. Code	Catfish Conc. (ppb)	Catfish Qual. Code	Crab Conc. (ppb)	Crab Qual. Code
EF052	ES	0.0455	U	44.377					
EF052	GE	0.0037		12.24		270.966		46.913	
EF052	NI	0.0047		63.96		609.656		73.909	
EF053	ES	0.0455	U	3.687					
EF054	ES	0.0455	U	43.793				8.689	
EF055	ES	0.0455	U	11.514					
EF056	ES	0.0455	U	118.384		263.258		73.305	
EF056	GE					115.351			
EF056	NI					371.715			
EF057	ES	0.0455	U	13.342		3.886		318.976	
EF057	GE	0.001	J	5.29		1201.887		500.722	
EF057	NI	0.009		9.92		2858.602			
EF058	ES	0.046	U	84.598		163.857		75.681	
EF058	GE					110.513			
EF058	NI					140.566			
EF059	ES	0.046	U						
EF060	ES	0.046	U						
EF061	ES	0.046	U	21.208		31.523		289.172	
EF061	GE	0.100		47.08		216.697		110.697	
EF061	NI	0.004		31.1		517.695		304.858	
EF062	ES	0.046	U	3.505					
EF064	ES	0.046	U	42.96					
HF029	GE			2.32	U			15.43	
HF030	ES	0.046	U	8.704		331.066		55.129	
HF030	GE	0.017		9.67		114.89		21.71	
HF030	NI	0.035		9.36		109.473		47.197	
HF031	GE			7.13				22.38	
HF032	GE			6.03				19.124	
HF034	GE			3.3				10.369	
HF035	ES							183.846	
HF035	GE			2.6				5.21	
HF035	NI							38.064	
HF037	ES	0.046	U	3.728		368.314		2.609	
HF037	GE	0.012		2.82		102.42		7.61	
HF037	NI	0.042		20.15		57.97		6.577	
HF038	GE			3.51				10.15	
HF039	GE			4.27				14.385	

Table 9. Total DDT results, cont.

Station	Lab	Water Conc. (ppb)	Water Qual. Code	Sediment Conc. (ppb)	Sediment Qual. Code	Catfish Conc. (ppb)	Catfish Qual. Code	Crab Conc. (ppb)	Crab Qual. Code
HF040	GE			7.51					
HF042	GE			2.53				18.468	
HF043	GE			1.77				21.405	
HF044	GE			1.08		32.172		17.037	
HF045	GE			3.37				17.931	
HF046	ES	0.0455	U	26.496		905.779			
HF046	GE	0.00383		14.27		283.91		32.25	
HF046	NI	0.01697		10.18		530.405			
HF047	GE			1.17					
HF048	GE			0.6	U	289.082		23.76	
HF049	GE			4.89				13.104	
HF050	GE			3.62		15.743		8.193	
HF051	GE			2.64				6.821	
HF063	GE			4.58				10.474	
HF065	GE			2.52					
NF011	ES					233.152			
NF011	GE					51.73			
NF011	NI	0.062		3.17		15.294		49.731	
NF012	NI	0.013		5.04					
NF013	ES	0.046	U	0.781	U			0.988	U
NF013	GE	0.002	J	3.32				46.73	
NF013	NI	0.003		7.16				21.289	
NF014	NI	0.017		3.24				24.093	
NF015	NI	0.003		5.57				43.924	
NF016	NI	0.002						38.725	
NF017	ES	0.046	U	11.032		18.422		39.414	
NF017	GE	0.003		4.97		153.39		70.81	
NF017	NI	0.003		9.3	·	200.869		69.003	
NF018	NI	0.017						104.857	
NF019	NI	0.002						95.44	
NF020	NI	0.031		0.85					
NF021	NI	0.026		2.23					
NF022	NI	0.006						37.966	
NF023	NI	0.005						45.718	
NF024	ES	0.046	U	9.344		498.926		16.862	
NF024	GE	0.006		3.46		147.89		29.16	
NF024	NI	0.052		4.05		635.965		45.925	
NF025	NI	0.005		31.39				26.861	

Table 9. Total DDT results, cont.

Station	Lab	Water		Sediment		Catfish		Crab	
		Conc. (ppb)	Qual. Code	Conc. (ppb)	Qual. Code	Conc. (ppb)	Qual. Code	Conc. (ppb)	Qual. Code
NF026	NI					11.18		101.669	
NF027	NI	0.014				4.16			
NF028	NI	0.024				9.54			

J   estimated concentration
U   below detection limit (concentration is detection limit)
ES   FUSADES
GE   Texas A&M
HO   CESCCO
NI   MAGFOR
N/A   not analyzed